F/Ko
K

1000 Ideas
For Color Schemes

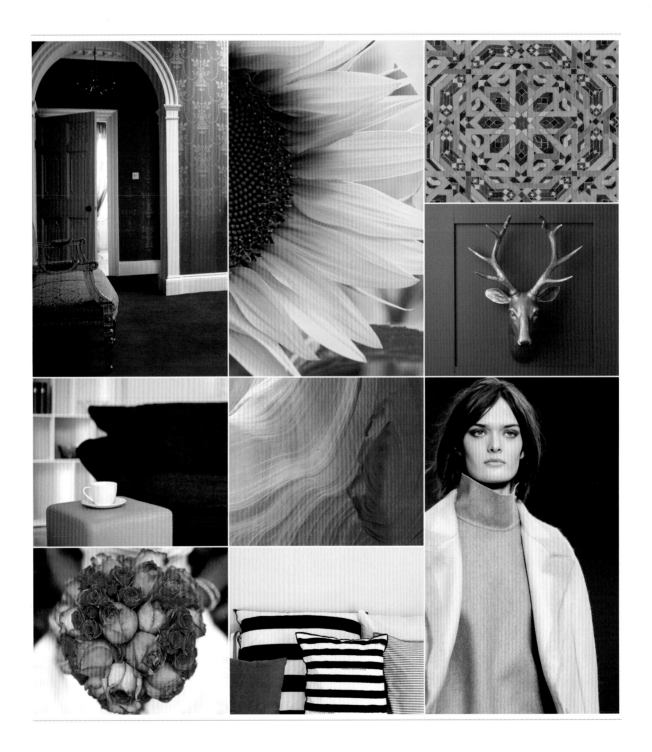

1000 Ideas
For Color Schemes

The ultimate guide to making colors work

Jennifer Ott

FIREFLY BOOKS

A FIREFLY BOOK

Published by Firefly Books Ltd. 2016

Copyright © 2016 Quarto Inc

First printing

Publisher Cataloging-in-Publication Data (U.S.)

Names: Ott, Jennifer, author.
Title: 1000 ideas for color schemes : the ultimate guide to making colors work / Jennifer Ott.
Description: Richmond Hill, Ontario, Canada : Firefly Books, 2016. |
Summary: "This guide contains 300 beautiful color palettes to help readers choose complementary colors for their living spaces, clothing, and food. Categorized into major color groups, the palettes are shown in reds, blues, greens, and others" — Provided by publisher.
Identifiers: ISBN 978-1-77085-752-0 (paperback)
Subjects: LCSH: Color in design.
Classification: LCC NK1548.O88 |DDC 701.85 – dc23

Library and Archives Canada Cataloguing in Publication

Ott, Jennifer, author   ⟨B⟩
        1000 ideas for color schemes : the ultimate guide to making colors work / Jennifer Ott.
ISBN 978-1-77085-752-0 (paperback)
        1. Color decoration and ornament. 2. Color guides. I. Title. II. Title: One thousand ideas for color schemes.
NK1548.O87 2016   701'.85   C2016-902022-3

Published in the United States by   Published in Canada by
Firefly Books (U.S.) Inc.   Firefly Books Ltd.
P.O. Box 1338, Ellicott Station   50 Staples Avenue, Unit 1
Buffalo, New York 14205   Richmond Hill, Ontario L4B 0A7

Color separation in Hong Kong by Bright Arts Ltd
Printed in China by C & C Offset Printing Co Ltd

Conceived, edited and designed by
Quarto Publishing plc
The Old Brewery
6 Blundell Street
London N7 9BH

Senior Editor: Lily de Gatacre
Picture Researcher: Mahina Drew
Proofreader: Caroline West
Indexer: Helen Snaith
Art Director: Caroline Guest
Creative Director: Moira Clinch
Publisher: Paul Carslake

Introduction   **012**
Using this Book   **014**

Black, White, and Red
All Over   **018**

Opposites Attract
                                      026

Tawny Tones
                                      034

Hint of Red
                                      042

The Sun in the Sky
                                      052

Cool with Yellow
                                      060

Contents

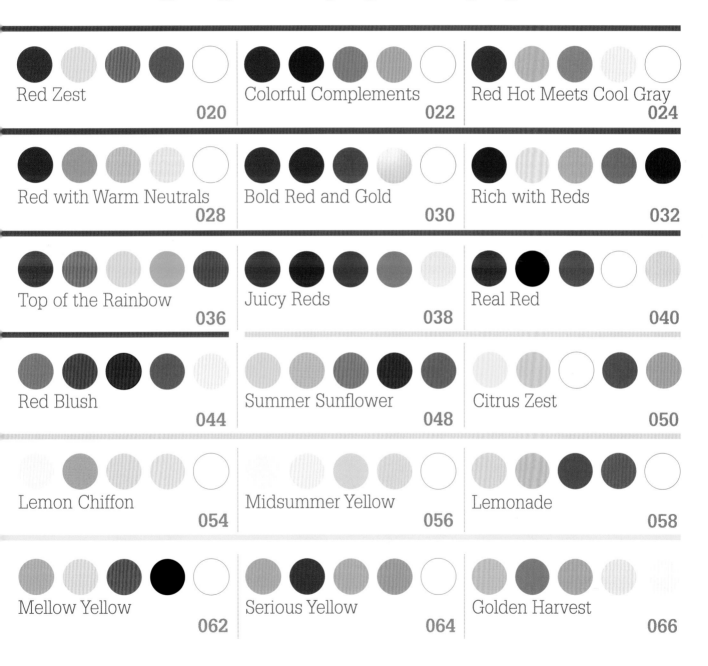

Red Zest
020

Colorful Complements
022

Red Hot Meets Cool Gray
024

Red with Warm Neutrals
028

Bold Red and Gold
030

Rich with Reds
032

Top of the Rainbow
036

Juicy Reds
038

Real Red
040

Red Blush
044

Summer Sunflower
048

Citrus Zest
050

Lemon Chiffon
054

Midsummer Yellow
056

Lemonade
058

Mellow Yellow
062

Serious Yellow
064

Golden Harvest
066

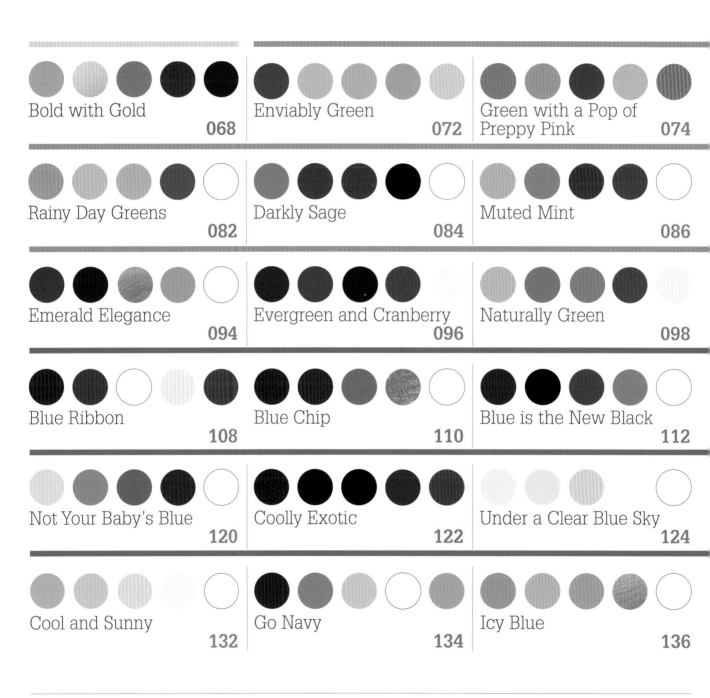

Bold with Gold
068

Enviably Green
072

Green with a Pop of Preppy Pink
074

Rainy Day Greens
082

Darkly Sage
084

Muted Mint
086

Emerald Elegance
094

Evergreen and Cranberry
096

Naturally Green
098

Blue Ribbon
108

Blue Chip
110

Blue is the New Black
112

Not Your Baby's Blue
120

Coolly Exotic
122

Under a Clear Blue Sky
124

Cool and Sunny
132

Go Navy
134

Icy Blue
136

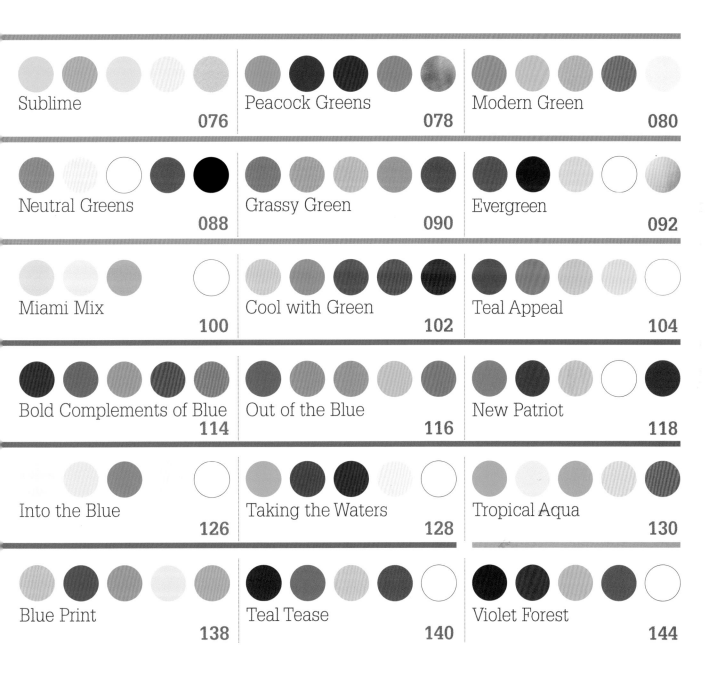

Sublime 076

Peacock Greens 078

Modern Green 080

Neutral Greens 088

Grassy Green 090

Evergreen 092

Miami Mix 100

Cool with Green 102

Teal Appeal 104

Bold Complements of Blue 114

Out of the Blue 116

New Patriot 118

Into the Blue 126

Taking the Waters 128

Tropical Aqua 130

Blue Print 138

Teal Tease 140

Violet Forest 144

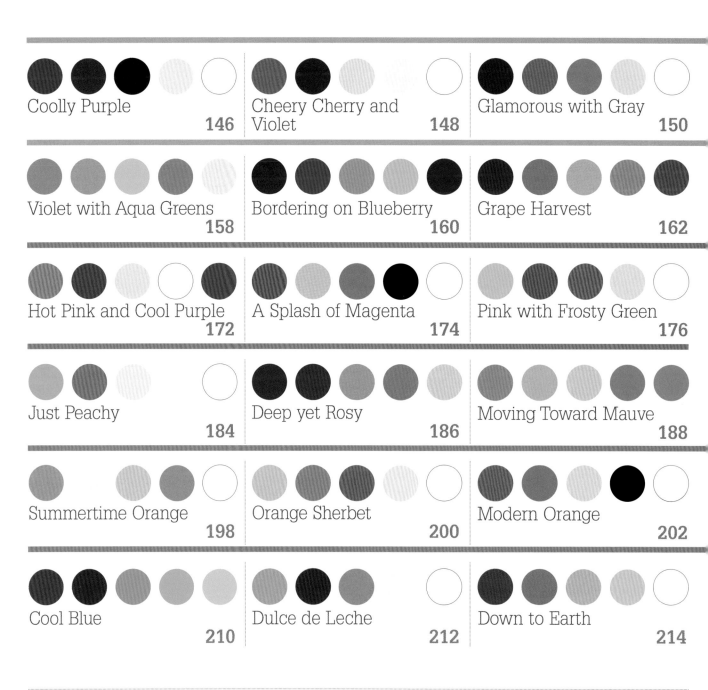

Coolly Purple 146

Cheery Cherry and Violet 148

Glamorous with Gray 150

Violet with Aqua Greens 158

Bordering on Blueberry 160

Grape Harvest 162

Hot Pink and Cool Purple 172

A Splash of Magenta 174

Pink with Frosty Green 176

Just Peachy 184

Deep yet Rosy 186

Moving Toward Mauve 188

Summertime Orange 198

Orange Sherbet 200

Modern Orange 202

Cool Blue 210

Dulce de Leche 212

Down to Earth 214

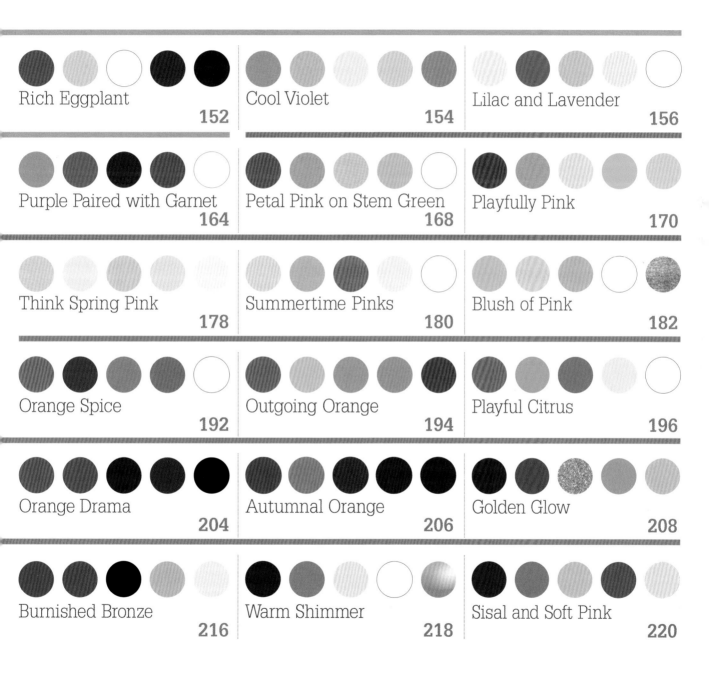

Rich Eggplant
152

Cool Violet
154

Lilac and Lavender
156

Purple Paired with Garnet
164

Petal Pink on Stem Green
168

Playfully Pink
170

Think Spring Pink
178

Summertime Pinks
180

Blush of Pink
182

Orange Spice
192

Outgoing Orange
194

Playful Citrus
196

Orange Drama
204

Autumnal Orange
206

Golden Glow
208

Burnished Bronze
216

Warm Shimmer
218

Sisal and Soft Pink
220

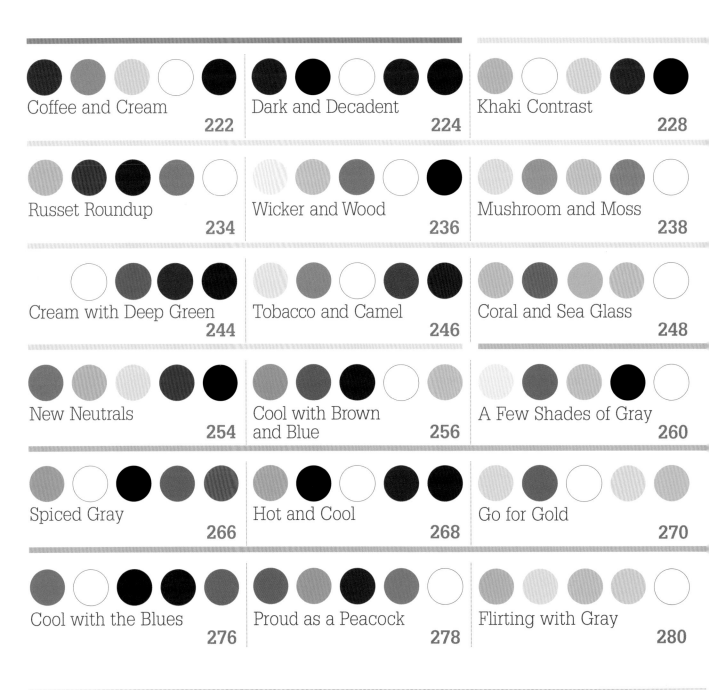

Coffee and Cream 222

Dark and Decadent 224

Khaki Contrast 228

Russet Roundup 234

Wicker and Wood 236

Mushroom and Moss 238

Cream with Deep Green 244

Tobacco and Camel 246

Coral and Sea Glass 248

New Neutrals 254

Cool with Brown and Blue 256

A Few Shades of Gray 260

Spiced Gray 266

Hot and Cool 268

Go for Gold 270

Cool with the Blues 276

Proud as a Peacock 278

Flirting with Gray 280

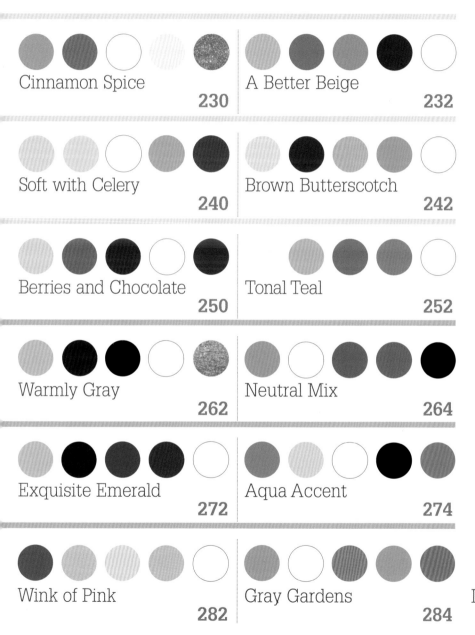

Cinnamon Spice
230

A Better Beige
232

Soft with Celery
240

Brown Butterscotch
242

Berries and Chocolate
250

Tonal Teal
252

Warmly Gray
262

Neutral Mix
264

Exquisite Emerald
272

Aqua Accent
274

Wink of Pink
282

Gray Gardens
284

Index and Credits
286

"There are no ugly colors; there are, however, many unappealing color combinations."

This is the single best piece of insight on color I've ever heard.

It was uttered by a former design mentor of mine while we were evaluating a renovation project in the Hollywood Hills. This was an A-list celebrity's home, but the previous owner's choice of paint colors was decidedly D-list. My mentor was correct, though, that although the bright green window trim was not quite the right shade to pair with the gold stucco, taken separately these were two perfectly lovely colors. I learned a great thing that day — that the trick to successfully working with color is to make sure the various hues in the scheme work together as a whole, rather than focusing solely on any individual color.

My obsession with color goes all the way back to my early childhood. I lobbied my mother hard at the beginning of each school year for the biggest box of crayons I could lay my hands on (all those glorious colors!). Never a highly skilled illustrator, I nonetheless loved creating little abstract drawings, using whichever colors happened to be my current favorites.

Once in college I couldn't wait to move out of the dormitory and into my very own apartment that I could furnish to my heart's desire. When my husband and I bought our first home together, a fixer-upper, we did most of the work ourselves and I discovered how color, via relatively inexpensive paint, could be used as a tool to enhance or disguise elements in a home.

I so thoroughly enjoyed the process of transforming an unattractive, dysfunctional property into a beautiful, color-filled home that I enrolled in the interior architecture program at the University of California, Los Angeles. Upon completion I began taking on interior design clients and quickly discovered a huge demand for design professionals willing to take on smaller jobs — such as color consultations. My long-held interest in, and experience with color served me well; I was able to carve out a niche for myself assisting homeowners with improving the interior and exterior of their homes through the creative use of color and materials.

I currently live in San Francisco with my husband and our two cats in yet another fixer-upper. In addition to running my own design firm, I also write color and interior design articles for various publications.

Jennifer Ott

Using this Book

This book is for anyone who loves color and is looking for creative palettes they can incorporate into their surroundings, whether for home décor and apparel, or special events, parties and weddings.

Sometimes you have an idea for a color combination and just need to see a real-life example of the palette in action to make sure it works. Or perhaps you love a specific hue but are unsure how to pair it with other colors to make it sing. Use this book to inspire you to think beyond the typical color combinations. Whether or not you've got a specific color in mind, use the visual contents on pages 4–11 to find a palette that jumps out at you and then locate it in the book. The ideas are grouped into nine main color families to give you some guidance, but the classifications are very fluid. When choosing a color scheme, you don't have to stick to all of the colors that are shown in the palette. You might find a scheme that you love exactly as it is, which is great, but there's nothing wrong with tweaking and editing the color palettes, using them as inspiration, or focusing on just two or three of the colors to create something wonderful.

Alongside this book, get color inspiration by collecting and organizing examples of the colorful things you love. Whether it's swatches of paint or fabrics, or images culled from magazines or online sources, just clip and save what you're drawn to. You'll likely find a theme running through these assembled items, whether it's a specific color or group of colors, a pattern or a material. Use these as the springboard from which you can further develop the color scheme or design.

The Color Wheel

This book requires no knowledge of color theory but a few basics about the color wheel will help. For the purposes of this book we are referring to color as it relates to paints, inks and dyes, rather than color as a projection of light — such as how you see it on your computer monitor or television. When referring to pigments, then, there are three **primary colors:** red, yellow and blue. From these three primaries we can mix the **secondary colors** of orange, green and violet. Additionally there are **tertiary colors** mixed from the primaries and secondaries: red-orange, yellow-orange, yellow-green, blue-green, blue-violet and red-violet. These twelve colors form the basic color wheel.

Complementary colors are colors that are opposite one another on the color wheel, the main combinations being blue and orange; red and green;

Color Selection Tip:

Most paint retailers can create a custom color blend for you, so if you see a color in this book that you would like translated into paint, simply bring this book in to have the swatch color-matched. Before committing to any paint color it's always a good idea to paint up a test swatch to evaluate the hue in your own space, during different times of the day.

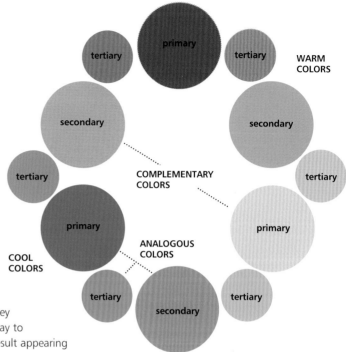

and yellow and violet. They offer the maximum amount of contrast to one another, and each makes the other appear more vibrant. This tension creates an energetic, dynamic color combination. **Analogous colors** are hues that sit next to one another on the color wheel. They tend to offer a pleasing, harmonious vibe and are a great way to employ an assortment of different colors without the end result appearing too garish. An example of an analogous color scheme is one inspired by the sea, featuring various shades of blue, blue-green and green.

A couple of other characteristics of color to consider are value and chroma. **Value** refers to the relative lightness or darkness of a color. When white is added to a hue it is said to be a high value color, and is referred to as a **tint**. Add black to a hue to create a **shade**, a low-value color. When gray is added to a hue it creates a mid-value color, and is referred to as a **tone**. **Chroma**, also known as intensity or saturation, has to do with the purity of color. A blue with a good amount of gray in it is going to appear much less saturated than pure primary blue. You can also desaturate a color by mixing in a small bit of its complement. Low-saturation colors tend to have a more natural and subdued quality to them.

Finally, you'll often see color in this book referred to as either "warm" or "cool." The **cool hues** on the color wheel run from yellow-green to violet. These hues have a calming, relaxing vibe. They also tend to visually recede, so when used in the home they can make a room feel larger and more expansive. The **warm colors** run from red-violet to yellow. These are happy, high-energy colors. In a home's interior they visually advance and can make a space feel more cozy and intimate.

"Use this book to inspire you to think beyond the typical color combinations."

red

Black, White, and Red All Over

Give a classic black and white scheme a boost through the addition of lush reds. Keep things light and bright by using white or light gray as the main color. If you prefer a bold, graphic look, up the red or black elements.

RED

YELLOW

GREEN

BLUE

VIOLET

PINK

ORANGE & BROWN

NEUTRAL

GRAY

Red Zest

Spicy, citrusy hues are a natural fit with red. These colors are all adjacent to one another on the warmer side of the color wheel, so although they are wildly colorful, they also have a harmonious flavor when used together.

RED

YELLOW

GREEN

BLUE

VIOLET

PINK

ORANGE
& BROWN

NEUTRAL

GRAY

Colorful Complements

This festive palette features complementary colors red and green. When working with complementary hues, it's a good idea to use one of the colors in small doses, or pick a muted version of it, so that the hues don't fight with one another.

RED
YELLOW
GREEN
BLUE
VIOLET
PINK
ORANGE & BROWN
NEUTRAL
GRAY

Red Hot Meets Cool Gray

Chill out with red by giving it a gray counterpoint. This mix of hot and cool feels balanced, ultramodern and very sophisticated. Select sparkling pewter or silver elements for an especially elegant touch.

RED

YELLOW

GREEN

BLUE

VIOLET

PINK

ORANGE
& BROWN

NEUTRAL

GRAY

Opposites Attract

Red-orange and blue-green are complementary colors, or opposites on the color wheel, so they amp up each other's vibrancy. Pairing these contrasting hues with black and white produces a youthful, high-octane, attention-grabbing palette.

RED

YELLOW

GREEN

BLUE

VIOLET

PINK

ORANGE
& BROWN

NEUTRAL

GRAY

Red with Warm Neutrals

True red is truly bold, but if you pair it with fellow warm hues, especially those of the soft, neutral variety, you can tone down the impact of the revved-up red. A touch of soft gray gives the palette a modern edge.

RED

YELLOW

GREEN

BLUE

VIOLET

PINK

ORANGE
& BROWN

NEUTRAL

GRAY

Bold Red and Gold

Red represents strength, vigor and passion, whereas gold conveys optimism, success and extravagance. When used in concert, the two make a powerful statement. Both are strong hues, so use one more sparingly than the other.

RED

YELLOW

GREEN

BLUE

VIOLET

PINK

ORANGE
& BROWN

NEUTRAL

GRAY

Rich with Reds

Red-wine hues get an indulgent kiss of caramel in this handsome color scheme.
It's the perfect palette for a bedroom or dining room — where a cozy and intimate
ambience is desired. In fashion, the hues convey a sophisticated and confident vibe.

RED

YELLOW

GREEN

BLUE

VIOLET

PINK

ORANGE
& BROWN

NEUTRAL

GRAY

Tawny Tones

These handsome, toned-down reds have strong brown and orange undertones, which give them a neutral quality. A rich and spicy palette like this works well for autumn occasions, or for décor in homes located in cold climates.

RED

YELLOW

GREEN

BLUE

VIOLET

PINK

ORANGE
& BROWN

NEUTRAL

GRAY

Top of the Rainbow

This colorful palette shouts with glee and calls for a party. Use it when a fun and lighthearted look is in order. It's a delightful scheme for a child's recreational space, or send it outside to play in the sunshine, which helps moderate the vividness.

RED

YELLOW

GREEN

BLUE

VIOLET

PINK

ORANGE
& BROWN

NEUTRAL

GRAY

Juicy Reds

Succulent strawberry, cherry and raspberry reds form a deliciously decadent palette. Such luscious colors pair well with a darker, punctuating hue such as crisp blue-gray. A dash of spring green lends a fresh element.

RED

YELLOW

GREEN

BLUE

VIOLET

PINK

ORANGE
& BROWN

NEUTRAL

GRAY

Real Red

A high-saturation red hue is sexy, exciting and always eye-catching. Allow it to take center stage by pairing it with solid, supporting neutrals. Black, dark gray, warm white and pure white hues form a solid foundation from which red can really sizzle.

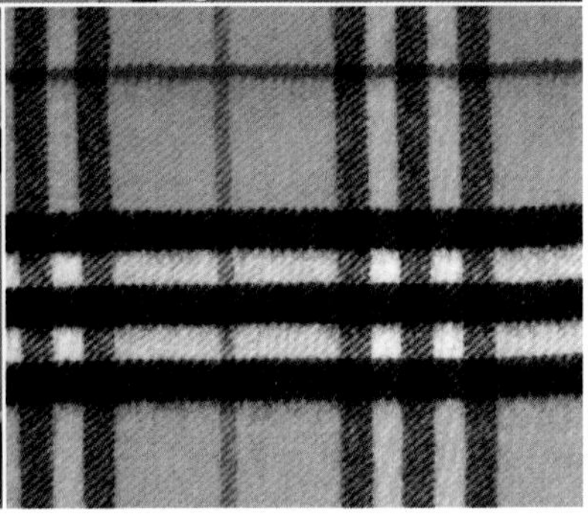

RED
YELLOW
GREEN
BLUE
VIOLET
PINK
ORANGE & BROWN
NEUTRAL
GRAY

Hint of Red

Tame an aggressive hue such as red either by using it in small amounts or by selecting a less-saturated version of it. Red tints (red with white added), tones (red with gray added) and shades (red with black added) have a softer quality than true red.

RED

YELLOW

GREEN

BLUE

VIOLET

PINK

ORANGE & BROWN

NEUTRAL

GRAY

Red Blush

Soft and slightly faded red-orange colors have a timeless elegance. These subdued copper and terracotta hues flatter a variety of skin tones, so they form a pleasing color scheme to surround oneself with, whether through fashion or décor.

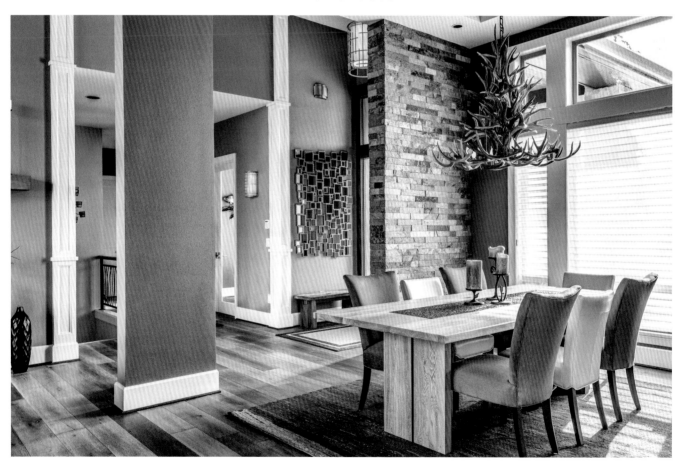

RED
YELLOW
GREEN
BLUE
VIOLET
PINK
ORANGE & BROWN
NEUTRAL
GRAY

yellow

Summer Sunflower

Vivid yellows and oranges join forces with a deep maroon and leafy green for a color scheme inspired by late-summer flowers. This is a lively palette that conjures up happy, joyful times.

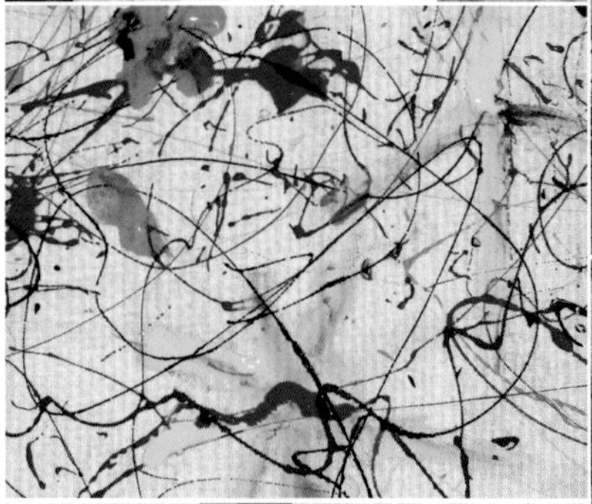

RED

YELLOW

GREEN

BLUE

VIOLET

PINK

ORANGE
& BROWN

NEUTRAL

GRAY

Citrus Zest

Turn to nature for a pleasing and stress-easing color palette. Whether inspired by the flowers in bloom or a display of fresh produce at the market, these big juicy colors delight the senses.

RED

YELLOW

GREEN

BLUE

VIOLET

PINK

ORANGE
& BROWN

NEUTRAL

GRAY

The Sun in the Sky

Yellow suggests warm sunshine and these deep blue hues evoke the sea and the sky. When used together, these near-complementary colors pulled from the great outdoors form a fun and dynamic palette.

RED

YELLOW

GREEN

BLUE

VIOLET

PINK

ORANGE
& BROWN

NEUTRAL

GRAY

Lemon Chiffon

Yellow can be tough to work with because it often comes on a bit too strong. Soften the impact by going with a tint — a yellow with white added. Muted yellow tints often work as neutrals in a color palette.

RED

YELLOW

GREEN

BLUE

VIOLET

PINK

ORANGE
& BROWN

NEUTRAL

GRAY

Midsummer Yellow

Transport yourself to the beach or poolside with a relaxed, sun-faded color scheme. Yellow should be the cornerstone of any summer-themed palette. A soft sorbet yellow paired with mint and a touch of cooling blue is sublime.

RED
YELLOW
GREEN
BLUE
VIOLET
PINK
ORANGE
& BROWN
NEUTRAL
GRAY

Lemonade

Take a refreshing sip of this sweet and tart hue. Yellows with green undertones bring a fresh and crisp vibe. They balance out heavier, murkier colors such as rum-raisin reds and deep emerald greens.

RED

YELLOW

GREEN

BLUE

VIOLET

PINK

ORANGE
& BROWN

NEUTRAL

GRAY

Cool with Yellow

A simple, cool and elegant palette starts with a base layer of gray and black. From here you can jazz it up with a splash of electric yellow. Such dazzling yellows are best in small doses and partnered with neutrals.

RED

YELLOW

GREEN

BLUE

VIOLET

PINK

ORANGE & BROWN

NEUTRAL

GRAY

Mellow Yellow

Bring the vibrancy level down by selecting yellows that have a bit of gray or brown in them, which keeps them from appearing fluorescent. Adding red, white and black to the palette gives it a punchy, graphic vibe.

RED

YELLOW

GREEN

BLUE

VIOLET

PINK

ORANGE
& BROWN

NEUTRAL

GRAY

Serious Yellow

Mustard yellow can be tricky to pull off due to its heavy brown undertones. Give it a fresh and modern boost by pairing it with steely blue-grays, as well as a healthy smattering of white.

RED

YELLOW

GREEN

BLUE

VIOLET

PINK

ORANGE
& BROWN

NEUTRAL

GRAY

Golden Harvest

As yellow shifts to orange it takes on a soft glow reminiscent of the setting sun or ready-to-harvest wheat fields. Warm browns, tans and creams serve as supporting neutrals in this luminous color scheme.

RED

YELLOW

GREEN

BLUE

VIOLET

PINK

ORANGE
& BROWN

NEUTRAL

GRAY

Bold with Gold

This warm, rich palette features fall's best hues. It's an ideal color scheme for places and spaces in which a cozy, welcoming vibe is desired. Counteract the heaviness of the dark brown hues by including sparkling gold elements.

RED

YELLOW

GREEN

BLUE

VIOLET

PINK

ORANGE
& BROWN

NEUTRAL

GRAY

green

Enviably Green

This fun, bold palette has an exotic vibe that is sure to spark a party atmosphere. Whether you are looking to stimulate appetites, conversations or good times, this tropically inspired scheme will keep the mood festive.

RED

YELLOW

GREEN

BLUE

VIOLET

PINK

ORANGE
& BROWN

NEUTRAL

GRAY

Green with a Pop of Preppy Pink

Pink and leafy green are complementary colors — opposite each other on the color wheel. This means they offer the most contrast to one another. The best way to punch up a yellow-green scheme is with a little pop of pink.

RED
YELLOW
GREEN
BLUE
VIOLET
PINK
ORANGE & BROWN
NEUTRAL
GRAY

Sublime

Lime is a vibrant yellow-green that can stand all on its own or have its impact softened by a pairing with other more herbaceous greens, as well as a generous dose of soft blue-grays.

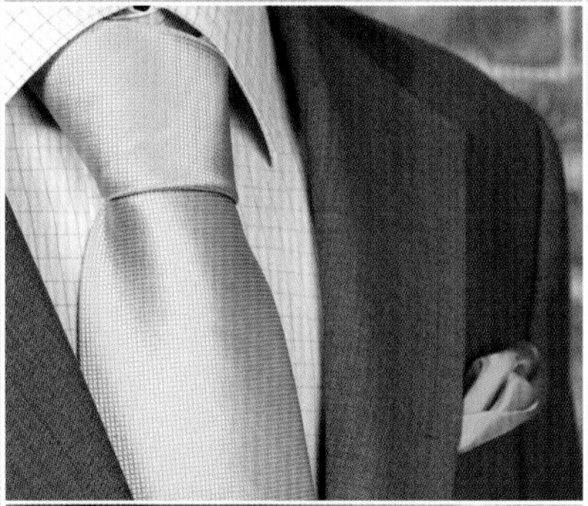

RED

YELLOW

GREEN

BLUE

VIOLET

PINK

ORANGE
& BROWN

NEUTRAL

GRAY

Peacock Greens

Rich, peacock-inspired greens and blues form a bold, fashionable color palette. There's nothing soft and neutral about this scheme, so use it to call attention to items that are worth putting in the limelight.

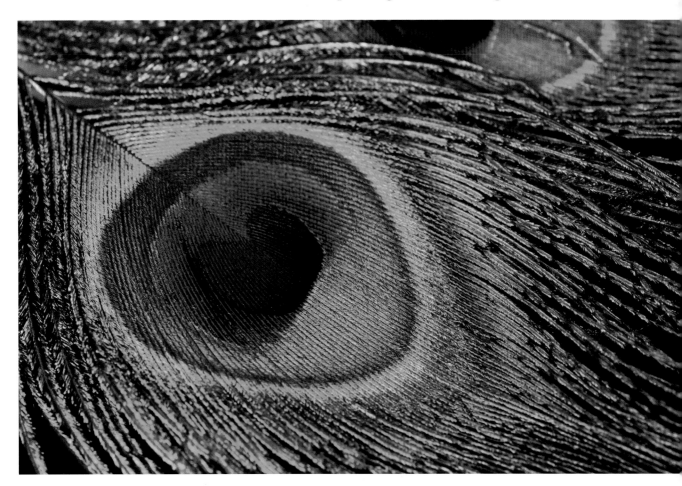

RED
YELLOW
GREEN
BLUE
VIOLET
PINK
ORANGE & BROWN
NEUTRAL
GRAY

Modern Green

Saturated greens play well with punchy citrus hues. It's a popular midcentury modern palette that continuously cycles back into vogue. These vibrant hues work best when one or two colors dominate, with the rest used as smaller accents.

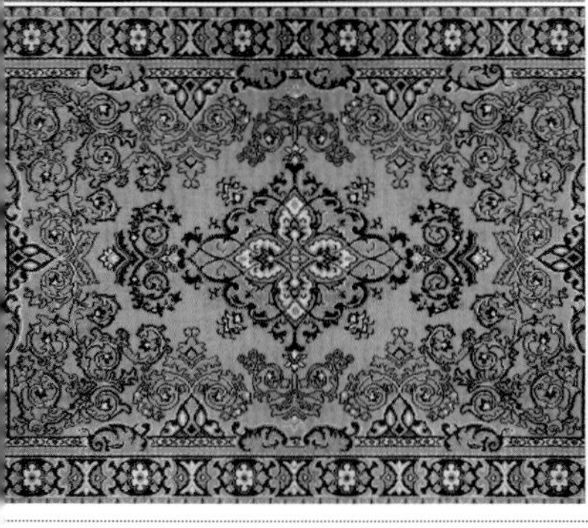

RED

YELLOW

GREEN

BLUE

VIOLET

PINK

ORANGE
& BROWN

NEUTRAL

GRAY

Rainy Day Greens

Blue-green hues call to mind water, and when they have a touch of gray in them they acquire a restful and almost moody quality. Sharpen them up with accents of darker blue and pure white.

RED

YELLOW

GREEN

BLUE

VIOLET

PINK

ORANGE
& BROWN

NEUTRAL

GRAY

Darkly Sage

A cool green with a heavy gray undertone can be used as an alternative to the cast of usual neutrals — white, gray and beige. You can pair pretty much any color you want with these dialed-down greens, making them super versatile.

RED

YELLOW

GREEN

BLUE

VIOLET

PINK

ORANGE
& BROWN

NEUTRAL

GRAY

Muted Mint

This featured green has a good amount of gray in it, which softens and neutralizes it. When partnered with a rich mahogany and a dark carbon gray, it forms a palette that is down-to-earth yet super elegant.

RED

YELLOW

GREEN

BLUE

VIOLET

PINK

ORANGE
& BROWN

NEUTRAL

GRAY

Neutral Greens

Soft greens with a generous dose of either gray or brown can stand on their own as a neutral hue, or you can pair them with other neutrals for a palette that is toned down yet layered and interesting.

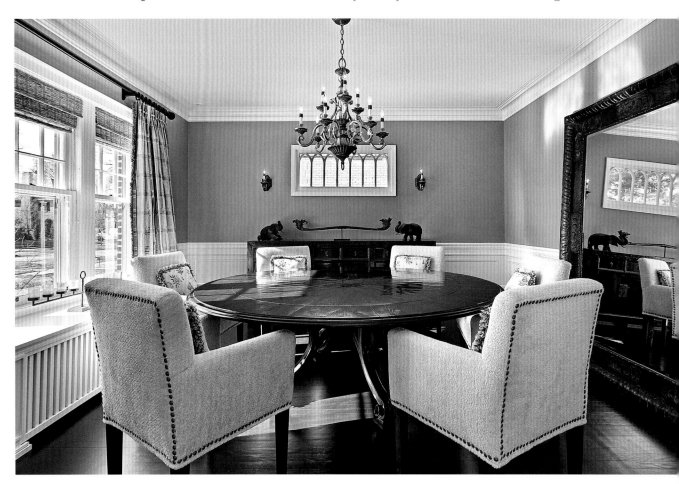

RED

YELLOW

GREEN

BLUE

VIOLET

PINK

ORANGE
& BROWN

NEUTRAL

GRAY

Grassy Green

Fresh greens taken from nature have a youthful vibrancy. We associate them with hope, rebirth and renewal, so we tend to be drawn to them during times of crisis or uncertainty in the world.

RED
YELLOW
GREEN
BLUE
VIOLET
PINK
ORANGE & BROWN
NEUTRAL
GRAY

Evergreen

These deep, dark, saturated greens need to be partnered with plenty of white or other light neutrals to keep the palette from becoming too somber or heavy. But in small quantities, they look absolutely dashing.

RED   YELLOW   GREEN   BLUE   VIOLET   PINK   ORANGE & BROWN   NEUTRAL   GRAY

Emerald Elegance

Dark and subdued, but in no way somber, this deep, dark green makes a nice
alternative to basic black or navy as the anchoring hue in a palette. Pair it with
a rich red wine or camel hue to give the scheme a warm boost.

RED

YELLOW

GREEN

BLUE

VIOLET

PINK

ORANGE
& BROWN

NEUTRAL

GRAY

Evergreen and Cranberry

True green and deep red are opposite one another on the color wheel and therefore each magnifies the intensity of the other. This palette is a bit of an attention-grabber, but the deep and saturated quality of the hues offers a comforting vibe.

RED

YELLOW

GREEN

BLUE

VIOLET

PINK

ORANGE
& BROWN

NEUTRAL

GRAY

Naturally Green

Greens with strong yellow and brown undertones feel very earthy and grounded. Layer them with other colors pulled from nature for a colorful yet soothing look, or jazz them up with splashes of more vibrant hues.

RED

YELLOW

GREEN

BLUE

VIOLET

PINK

ORANGE & BROWN

NEUTRAL

GRAY

Miami Mix

Not quite pastels, but also not fully saturated brights, these are colors that have been softened by exposure to the sun and salt air. This fun palette evokes warm sunny days near the beach and hot nights on the town.

RED
YELLOW
GREEN
BLUE
VIOLET
PINK
ORANGE & BROWN
NEUTRAL
GRAY

Cool with Green

For a colorful palette that retains a harmonious vibe, gather an assortment of colors from one end of the color spectrum. Here we have a range of cool colors from blue-green to purple-red that smoothly flow into one another.

RED
YELLOW
GREEN
BLUE
VIOLET
PINK
ORANGE & BROWN
NEUTRAL
GRAY

Teal Appeal

Teal and golden yellow aren't quite complementary colors, but they do contrast with one another so that they coalesce into an energetic, lively palette. Use one as a background to the other to set each element apart.

RED

YELLOW

GREEN

BLUE

VIOLET

PINK

ORANGE
& BROWN

NEUTRAL

GRAY

blue

Blue Ribbon

True blue colors tend to recede visually, so they make a great background hue that allows other warmer colors to advance. When used inside a home they can help make a space feel more spacious and open.

RED

YELLOW

GREEN

BLUE

VIOLET

PINK

ORANGE
& BROWN

NEUTRAL

GRAY

Blue Chip

Blue is associated with loyalty, trust and commitment. Gold elements call to mind wealth, opulence and decadence. This interesting combination of colors and meanings has an upscale, formal quality that evokes momentous occasions.

Blue is the New Black

Enhance the classic elegance of black and charcoal gray with the addition of inky indigo hues. Keep the scheme airy and light through the use of plenty of white and soft gray. For more drama, up the amount of deep, dark hues.

RED

YELLOW

GREEN

BLUE

VIOLET

PINK

ORANGE
& BROWN

NEUTRAL

GRAY

Bold Complements of Blue

Blue and orange are complementary colors, or color wheel contrasts. They are best used when an exciting, high-energy look is desired. One way to make it more mellow is to use one or both of the hues in small amounts only.

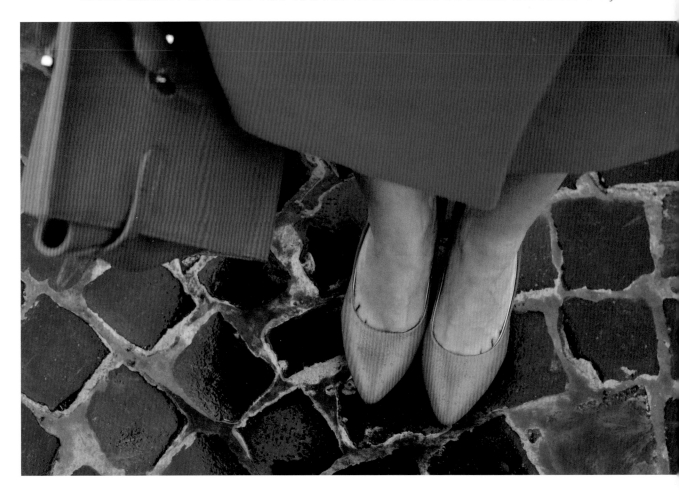

RED

YELLOW

GREEN

BLUE

VIOLET

PINK

ORANGE
& BROWN

NEUTRAL

GRAY

Out of the Blue

This palette is for enthusiastic lovers of color. A sampling of more than half of the color wheel (from orange to yellow to green to blue), it's a vivid scheme that should be reserved for occasions or items worthy of one's individual attention.

RED

YELLOW

GREEN

BLUE

VIOLET

PINK

ORANGE
& BROWN

NEUTRAL

GRAY

New Patriot

Red, white and blue comprise the colors of the flag of many countries. Replace the royal or navy blue with toned-down shades of gray-blue for a fresh take on the palette. It's an unexpected scheme that has an understated appeal.

RED

YELLOW

GREEN

BLUE

VIOLET

PINK

ORANGE
& BROWN

NEUTRAL

GRAY

Not Your Baby's Blue

If you prefer muted blues but don't want a palette of pastels, select blue tones (blue mixed with gray) or shades (blue mixed with black). The touch of gray or black softens the chroma, or purity, of the color, giving the colors more of a neutral quality.

RED

YELLOW

GREEN

BLUE

VIOLET

PINK

ORANGE
& BROWN

NEUTRAL

GRAY

Coolly Exotic

Hot pinks and cool blue-violets merge to form a hip, bohemian palette. This gorgeous scheme makes a striking statement. Use the bolder hues and the contrast between the colors to set off items worthy of being in the limelight.

RED

YELLOW

GREEN

BLUE

VIOLET

PINK

ORANGE
& BROWN

NEUTRAL

GRAY

Under a Clear Blue Sky

Light sky blues offer the gentlest wisp of color. To maintain a delicate touch, combine them with soft pastels such as pink and plenty of white. It's a sweet and innocent palette that's perfect for children's spaces and springtime celebrations.

RED

YELLOW

GREEN

BLUE

VIOLET

PINK

ORANGE
& BROWN

NEUTRAL

GRAY

Into the Blue

A generous helping of pretty soft blues has an airy and ethereal quality. When used in architectural applications, it exudes a cheerful sea- and sky-kissed vibe. In fashion and décor, it's fun and lighthearted, never to be taken too seriously.

RED

YELLOW

GREEN

BLUE

VIOLET

PINK

ORANGE
& BROWN

NEUTRAL

GRAY

Taking the Waters

Watery blue colors can help us feel calm, soothed and relaxed. Up the energy level by increasing the vibrancy of one or more of the blue hues. It will still have a replenishing vibe, just with a bit more pep.

RED

YELLOW

GREEN

BLUE

VIOLET

PINK

ORANGE
& BROWN

NEUTRAL

GRAY

Tropical Aqua

Bold blues with green undertones take us to warm and exotic places, especially when partnered with cheerful corals and pinks. This fun and vivacious color scheme is ready for a party.

RED

YELLOW

GREEN

BLUE

VIOLET

PINK

ORANGE
& BROWN

NEUTRAL

GRAY

Cool and Sunny

Pool-blue hues mixed with golden sunshine yellows take us outdoors for some summertime fun. This can be a rather bold palette when used inside the home. You can rein it in a bit by using one of the vibrant colors as a small accent only.

RED

YELLOW

GREEN

BLUE

VIOLET

PINK

ORANGE
& BROWN

NEUTRAL

GRAY

Go Navy

The darkest hues of blue have a handsome quality, but they can also feel a bit serious. Lighten them up with softer blue-grays and white. The addition of soft caramel or warm wood tones helps take the chill off.

RED

YELLOW

GREEN

BLUE

VIOLET

PINK

ORANGE & BROWN

NEUTRAL

GRAY

Icy Blue

Blue is a natural fit with cool gray hues and metallic silver elements. This palette can feel a bit cold, so it's the perfect choice for homes in hot climates. In fashion it has a luxurious and elegant air without veering toward heavy or severe.

RED

YELLOW

GREEN

BLUE

VIOLET

PINK

ORANGE
& BROWN

NEUTRAL

GRAY

Blue Print

Blue and green are side-by-side on the color wheel, so they play together nicely
due to their similarity. Mix up a batch of beautiful true blue and green-blue
colors for a subtly colorful palette.

RED

YELLOW

GREEN

BLUE

VIOLET

PINK

ORANGE
& BROWN

NEUTRAL

GRAY

Teal Tease

Deep blues with strong green undertones have an appealing, elegant air.
They're an excellent choice when a rich yet unconventional color is desired.
When paired with cool, steely grays, they give a youthful, modern vibe.

RED

YELLOW

GREEN

BLUE

VIOLET

PINK

ORANGE
& BROWN

NEUTRAL

GRAY

violet

Violet Forest

When working with bold, juicy purples, take inspiration from a bouquet of beautiful flowers and include plenty of leafy greens. These green hues bring a soothing organic vibe to the palette and help to ground the bright dashes of purple.

RED

YELLOW

GREEN

BLUE

VIOLET

PINK

ORANGE & BROWN

NEUTRAL

GRAY

Coolly Purple

A blue-tinged purple looks sharp when paired with classic navy. The colors are quite similar, so they flow into one another seamlessly. A splash of magenta adds warmth and vibrancy to the palette.

RED

YELLOW

GREEN

BLUE

VIOLET

PINK

ORANGE & BROWN

NEUTRAL

GRAY

Cheery Cherry and Violet

This is a rich, vibrant color palette, worthy of a special occasion. Balance out the bold purple and reds by adding a small dash of violet's complementary color: yellow. Some white space also provides a visual breather.

RED

YELLOW

GREEN

BLUE

VIOLET

PINK

ORANGE
& BROWN

NEUTRAL

GRAY

Glamorous with Gray

Flat gray hues tend to impart a modern, industrial vibe. Add a beguiling boost of lilac to the color scheme to soften it up and make it more special. Enhancing with texture and sheen will also bring this palette to life.

RED

YELLOW

GREEN

BLUE

VIOLET

PINK

ORANGE & BROWN

NEUTRAL

GRAY

Rich Eggplant

Deep, dark and dashing, this hue is a warmer alternative to black or navy. A soft, silvery lilac adds a layer of lightness that keeps the palette from feeling too heavy or somber.

RED

YELLOW

GREEN

BLUE

VIOLET

PINK

ORANGE
& BROWN

NEUTRAL

GRAY

Cool Violet

Violet, blue and green are analogous colors, meaning they are next to one another on the color wheel. Because of the similarity of hues, they feel harmonious when used together, despite the kaleidoscope of different colors.

RED

YELLOW

GREEN

BLUE

VIOLET

PINK

ORANGE
& BROWN

NEUTRAL

GRAY

Lilac and Lavender

Soft, soothing light violet hues are thought to reduce feelings of stress and anxiety, so they are a terrific choice for home interiors. In fashion they have a cool, ethereal quality that can either be dressed up or down.

RED

YELLOW

GREEN

BLUE

VIOLET

PINK

ORANGE
& BROWN

NEUTRAL

GRAY

Violet with Aqua Greens

Though not quite complementary colors, this collection of cool lilacs and violets with splashy aquas offers a vibrant palette option. This attention-getting scheme is best reserved for spaces, places and objects deserving of the spotlight.

RED

YELLOW

GREEN

BLUE

VIOLET

PINK

ORANGE
& BROWN

NEUTRAL

GRAY

Bordering on Blueberry

Bold hues can sometimes fight with one another, but these purples and greens all have strong blue undertones, so when partnered with true blue, they feel harmonious and cohesive despite the use of highly saturated colors.

RED
YELLOW
GREEN
BLUE
VIOLET
PINK
ORANGE
& BROWN
NEUTRAL
GRAY

Grape Harvest

Autumnal yellow-orange hues serve as a dramatic backdrop to deep grape colors. These nearly complementary hues sit in strong contrast to one another, forming a dynamic color scheme. Ease the energy level by including some toned-down violets.

RED

YELLOW

GREEN

BLUE

VIOLET

PINK

ORANGE & BROWN

NEUTRAL

GRAY

Purple Paired with Garnet

Gather up your favorite violet and red-violet hues for a beautiful, romantic color scheme. The deeper plum colors really stand out against the softer, silvery lavender hues without looking too busy or severe.

RED

YELLOW

GREEN

BLUE

VIOLET

PINK

ORANGE
& BROWN

NEUTRAL

GRAY

pink

Petal Pink on Stem Green

Look to nature for pink inspiration. Pretty petal pinks are right at home atop fresh, leafy greens. Pink and light green are complementary colors and, when used together, they pump up the vibrancy of one another.

RED
YELLOW
GREEN
BLUE
VIOLET
PINK
ORANGE & BROWN
NEUTRAL
GRAY

Playfully Pink

Red, blue and yellow are triadic colors — they are evenly spaced on the color wheel. They form a high-contrast, high-energy color palette. Using lighter shades of the hues will tone down the intensity of the palette while retaining the fun factor.

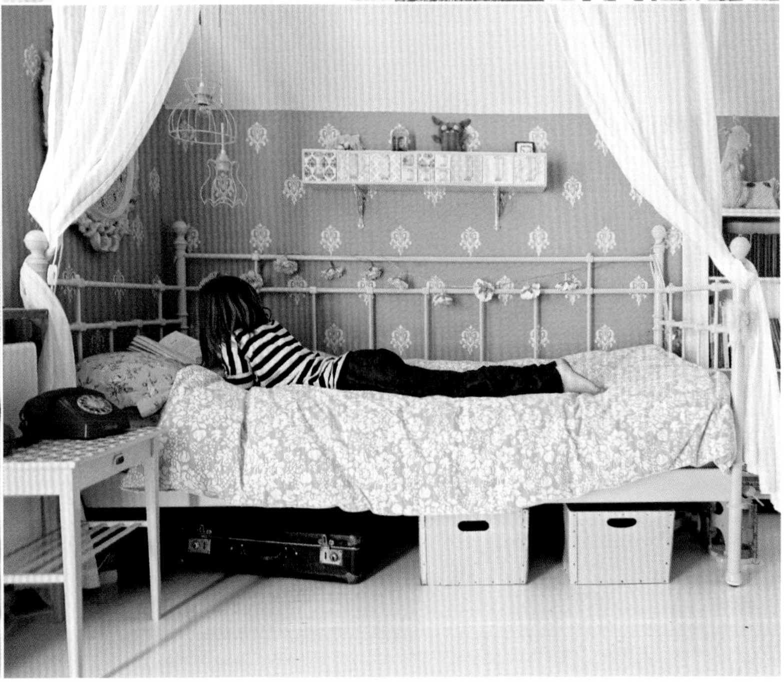

RED

YELLOW

GREEN

BLUE

VIOLET

PINK

ORANGE
& BROWN

NEUTRAL

GRAY

Hot Pink and Cool Purple

An assortment of pleasing pinks and purples unite for an enchanting color scheme. The saturated pink hues give the palette a sophisticated vibe, whereas softer pinks veer it toward a more youthful look.

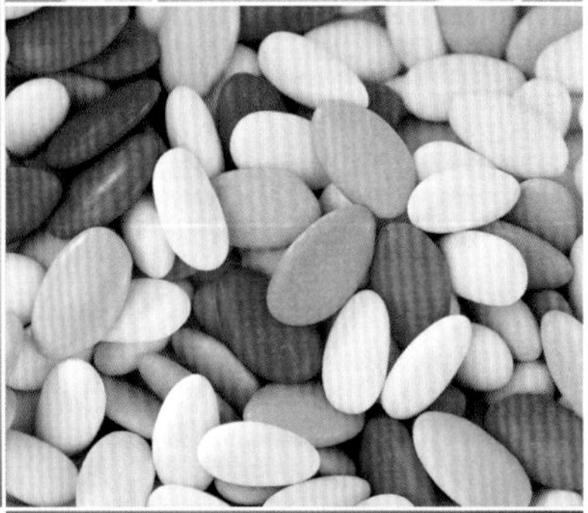

RED

YELLOW

GREEN

BLUE

VIOLET

PINK

ORANGE
& BROWN

NEUTRAL

GRAY

A Splash of Magenta

These pinks are not mere wallflower hues. So, although black and other dark neutrals can be used to form the basis of an elegant palette, a small injection of bold pink offers an unexpected boost of chic vivacity.

RED

YELLOW

GREEN

BLUE

VIOLET

PINK

ORANGE & BROWN

NEUTRAL

GRAY

Pink with Frosty Green

Layers of punchy pinks are always going to be the life of the party. Offer the eye a visual break by adding some contrasting silvery greens, then mix in plenty of white for a fetching palette that has a nice vintage feel.

RED

YELLOW

GREEN

BLUE

VIOLET

PINK

ORANGE
& BROWN

NEUTRAL

GRAY

Think Spring Pink

A rainbow of pretty pastels heralds springtime and its hopeful sentiments of rebirth and renewal. The key to making this palette work is to look for colors that are of a similar value (lightness or darkness) and tint (amount of white added to the hue).

RED

YELLOW

GREEN

BLUE

VIOLET

PINK

ORANGE
& BROWN

NEUTRAL

GRAY

Summertime Pinks

A batch of sweet pinks gets a warm boost from summer-sun yellow. This palette has a fun, youthful vibrancy. These are the happy hues of a season in full bloom and long days spent frolicking in the warm sunshine.

RED

YELLOW

GREEN

BLUE

VIOLET

PINK

ORANGE & BROWN

NEUTRAL

GRAY

Blush of Pink

A light seashell pink has a soft, breathy quality that you can make instantly elegant by pairing it with soft neutrals and metallic hues. A super-subtle palette such as this relies on interesting textiles to really make it sing.

RED

YELLOW

GREEN

BLUE

VIOLET

PINK

ORANGE
& BROWN

NEUTRAL

GRAY

Just Peachy

Fruit-inspired hues exude a sweet, comforting vibe. These pinks, peaches and soft yellows are analogous colors, so although they pack a punch, they do it in a harmonious way. Up the elegance factor by including sparkling silver or pearlescent elements.

RED

YELLOW

GREEN

BLUE

VIOLET

PINK

ORANGE
& BROWN

NEUTRAL

GRAY

Deep yet Rosy

Here's a pink-based color scheme for anyone looking to ditch the pastels. A rich, dark rose hue can work as a neutral in a colorful palette, especially when partnered with fellow toned-down colors.

RED
YELLOW
GREEN
BLUE
VIOLET
PINK
ORANGE
& BROWN
NEUTRAL
GRAY

Moving Toward Mauve

There's nothing babyish about this pink. A touch of gray knocks down the intensity, rendering it a little less sweet and innocent. This toned-down pink brings a welcome dash of warmth and spice to a palette full of similar moody, tonal hues.

RED

YELLOW

GREEN

BLUE

VIOLET

PINK

ORANGE
& BROWN

NEUTRAL

GRAY

orange

& brown

Orange Spice

These brown-tinged oranges are spicy yet earthy. A foolproof way to pick a pleasingly colorful orange scheme is to select oranges that are of a similar value (lightness or darkness) and chroma (purity of color).

RED

YELLOW

GREEN

BLUE

VIOLET

PINK

ORANGE
& BROWN

NEUTRAL

GRAY

Outgoing Orange

Colors on the warm side of the color wheel (reds, oranges and yellows) give off a friendly, vivacious vibe, especially the bolder versions. Warm colors are thought to encourage conversation so they are perfect for dining rooms and party décor.

RED

YELLOW

GREEN

BLUE

VIOLET

PINK

ORANGE & BROWN

NEUTRAL

GRAY

Playful Citrus

Herbaceous green can serve as a neutral, so don't be afraid to add a little orange zest to the mix. There's no need to go eye-searingly bold here; using more toned-down greens will balance out a fiery orange.

RED

YELLOW

GREEN

BLUE

VIOLET

PINK

ORANGE & BROWN

NEUTRAL

GRAY

Summertime Orange

Sun-faded colors have a soft, dreamy and pleasing quality. These aren't quite pastel hues, but rather the toned-down versions of the vibrant fresh fruit and floral colors of spring.

RED

YELLOW

GREEN

BLUE

VIOLET

PINK

ORANGE
& BROWN

NEUTRAL

GRAY

Orange Sherbet

A bold orange, although beautiful and eye-catching, can be a bit much when used in large doses. Try pairing it with light, creamy oranges, as well as a generous portion of white, to help balance out the brightness.

RED

YELLOW

GREEN

BLUE

VIOLET

PINK

ORANGE & BROWN

NEUTRAL

GRAY

Modern Orange

Orange hues are traditionally paired with warm neutrals such as tan, beige and cream. For a modern twist, try partnering orange with cooler neutrals such as taupe and gray, as well as cool whites and blacks.

RED

YELLOW

GREEN

BLUE

VIOLET

PINK

ORANGE
& BROWN

NEUTRAL

GRAY

Orange Drama

Inky blue-gray and basic black are handsome base colors that get a lively lift when combined with pumpkin orange. Tints and shades of red-violet soften the contrast and add a whimsical element.

RED

YELLOW

GREEN

BLUE

VIOLET

PINK

ORANGE
& BROWN

NEUTRAL

GRAY

Autumnal Orange

The warm, rich colors of the changing leaves herald the fall and a period of transition ahead. Keep the palette from getting too spooky by bringing in plenty of lively orange and red-orange hues.

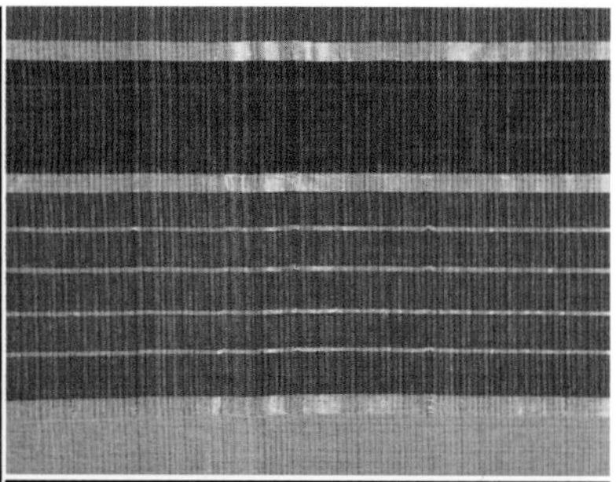

RED
YELLOW
GREEN
BLUE
VIOLET
PINK
ORANGE & BROWN
NEUTRAL
GRAY

Golden Glow

As orange veers toward brown it can start to turn a bit muddy. Perk it up with warm metallic accents such as copper, bronze and gold. These monochromatic color schemes are perfect for playing around with texture, sheen and pattern.

RED

YELLOW

GREEN

BLUE

VIOLET

PINK

ORANGE
& BROWN

NEUTRAL

GRAY

Cool Blue

Orange and blue are complementary colors, or opposite each other on the color wheel. When using complementary colors keep in mind that they each make the other appear more intense. Try keeping one of the hues more toned down, like this orange-brown if the other is vibrant like these turquoise shades.

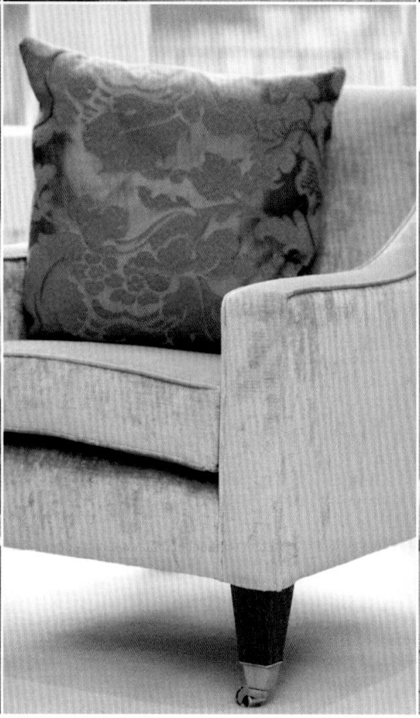

RED

YELLOW

GREEN

BLUE

VIOLET

PINK

ORANGE
& BROWN

NEUTRAL

GRAY

Dulce de Leche

Sweet caramel and butterscotch hues provide a tasty alternative to basic brown or black. Mix and match tints (color mixed with white), tones (color mixed with gray) and shades (color mixed with black) for a palette that's colorful but understated.

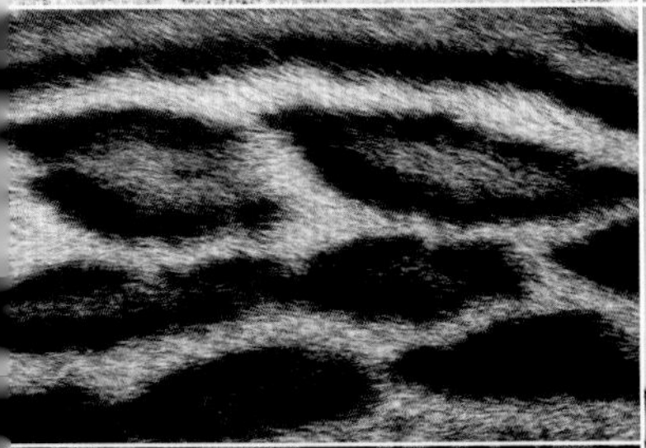

RED

YELLOW

GREEN

BLUE

VIOLET

PINK

ORANGE
& BROWN

NEUTRAL

GRAY

Down to Earth

Rich brown hues inspired by nature have a pleasing organic quality. From this earthy base, bring in a pretty accent such as a soft blushing pink. This particular pink has orange undertones, which keep it from going too sugary sweet.

RED

YELLOW

GREEN

BLUE

VIOLET

PINK

ORANGE
& BROWN

NEUTRAL

GRAY

Burnished Bronze

Balance out cool, steely grays with warm, blackened bronze hues. Mixing warm tones with cool neutrals is a terrific way to bust out of an all-gray or all-beige rut. You can then add just about any fun accent color that you like to this scheme.

RED

YELLOW

GREEN

BLUE

VIOLET

PINK

ORANGE
& BROWN

NEUTRAL

GRAY

Warm Shimmer

Typically, orange and brown hues are paired with warm metallic elements.
For a more modern approach, try partnering them with cool silver chromes
and steels. Polished metallic surfaces also amp up the elegance.

RED

YELLOW

GREEN

BLUE

VIOLET

PINK

ORANGE
& BROWN

NEUTRAL

GRAY

Sisal and Soft Pink

Colors pulled from natural fibers have a soft and casual quality, but with the added dash of shimmery pink, the palette takes on a dressier edge. It's an elegant palette that doesn't feel old or stuffy.

RED

YELLOW

GREEN

BLUE

VIOLET

PINK

ORANGE & BROWN

NEUTRAL

GRAY

Coffee and Cream

This beautiful palette starts with a foundation of rich coffee hues — from a deep, dark espresso to a light café au lait — to which a generous dose of purple plum is introduced. The effect is glamorous without being too showy.

RED
YELLOW
GREEN
BLUE
VIOLET
PINK
ORANGE & BROWN
NEUTRAL
GRAY

Dark and Decadent

Delicious dark chocolate hues provide a rich base layer for a splash of deep cherry red. This sophisticated scheme is perfect for a dining room, library or master bedroom — spaces in which a cozy and intimate atmosphere is desired.

RED
YELLOW
GREEN
BLUE
VIOLET
PINK
ORANGE
& BROWN
NEUTRAL
GRAY

neutral

Khaki Contrast

Take khaki tan and pair it with contrasting light and dark hues for a neutral palette that has plenty of variety. The white keeps it light, and the dashes of dark brown and black add depth.

RED

YELLOW

GREEN

BLUE

VIOLET

PINK

ORANGE & BROWN

NEUTRAL

GRAY

Cinnamon Spice

Softly spicy hues impart a cozy and comforting ambience. A soft and harmonious palette such as this can handle shimmering elements, so consider amping up the glamour factor with the addition of warm metallic tones.

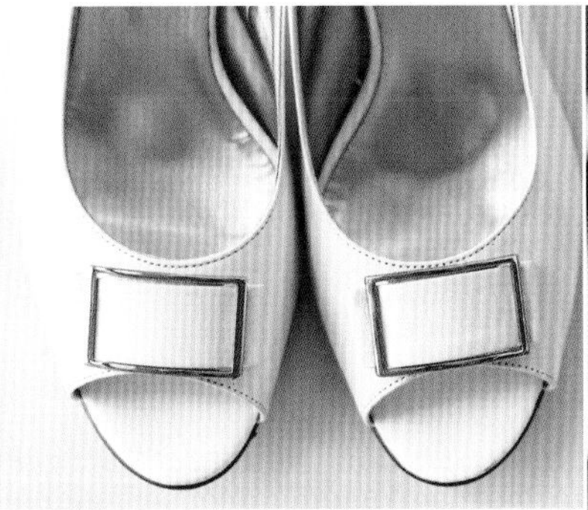

RED

YELLOW

GREEN

BLUE

VIOLET

PINK

ORANGE
& BROWN

NEUTRAL

GRAY

A Better Beige

If you aren't a fan of ubiquitous beige and tan but haven't fully embraced gray either, give cooler shades of beige and tan a chance. These contain more gray than their warmer counterparts, giving them a fresh and modern air.

RED

YELLOW

GREEN

BLUE

VIOLET

PINK

ORANGE
& BROWN

NEUTRAL

GRAY

Russet Roundup

Highly saturated shades of warm hues such as red, orange and yellow can be visually noisy and overwhelming, especially when used in a home's interior. For a softer, more comforting vibe, go for toned-down versions of these hues.

RED
YELLOW
GREEN
BLUE
VIOLET
PINK
ORANGE & BROWN
NEUTRAL
GRAY

Wicker and Wood

A mix of browns — light and dark as well as warm and cool — unite for a rich, timeless palette. When working with a nearly monochromatic palette such as this, consider playing up texture, pattern and sheen.

RED

YELLOW

GREEN

BLUE

VIOLET

PINK

ORANGE
& BROWN

NEUTRAL

GRAY

Mushroom and Moss

Nature arguably offers up some of the best color palettes. Soft green and taupe hues abound in the natural world and so we tend to attach positive associations to them when we encounter them in other contexts.

RED

YELLOW

GREEN

BLUE

VIOLET

PINK

ORANGE
& BROWN

NEUTRAL

GRAY

Soft with Celery

Shake up a light and neutral palette with the addition of a crisp green hue. Greens with strong yellow undertones lend a fresh and cheery note. They're vibrant colors but also rather light in value, meaning they don't overwhelm.

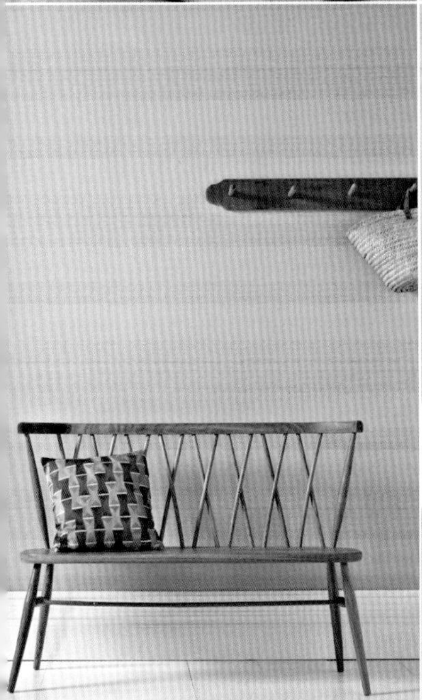

RED

YELLOW

GREEN

BLUE

VIOLET

PINK

ORANGE
& BROWN

NEUTRAL

GRAY

Brown Butterscotch

Predominantly white and off-white palettes have an airy and ethereal quality.
Ground the palette and add definition with the strategic inclusion of darker
hues, such as a rich brown or tonal orange.

RED

YELLOW

GREEN

BLUE

VIOLET

PINK

ORANGE & BROWN

NEUTRAL

GRAY

Cream with Deep Green

Bring green out of the deep, dark forest and into a more formal and light-filled setting by partnering it with warm whites. These greens have slight blue undertones; the coolness they impart contrasts nicely with the soft warmth of the creams.

RED

YELLOW

GREEN

BLUE

VIOLET

PINK

ORANGE
& BROWN

NEUTRAL

GRAY

Tobacco and Camel

These handsome, classic neutrals benefit from a nice wine pairing. The luscious burgundy color helps to temper the slight muddiness of the main neutral colors. To retain its sense of specialness, use the burgundy as a small accent only.

RED
YELLOW
GREEN
BLUE
VIOLET
PINK
ORANGE & BROWN
NEUTRAL
GRAY

Coral and Sea Glass

Colorful palettes need not be overly bold and boisterous. Stick to a variety of soft, weathered hues for a neutral take on a color-rich scheme. Dried-grass hues make a fantastic base for additional layers of soft coral and sea-glass green.

RED

YELLOW

GREEN

BLUE

VIOLET

PINK

ORANGE
& BROWN

NEUTRAL

GRAY

Berries and Chocolate

Surround yourself with the indulgent colors of your favorite comfort foods. Vanilla, chocolate and berry-red hues rev up the appetite and invigorate the senses, but they can also be used to add an air of contentment.

RED

YELLOW

GREEN

BLUE

VIOLET

PINK

ORANGE
& BROWN

NEUTRAL

GRAY

Tonal Teal

Light and warm neutrals such as beige and tan tend to be popular go-to hues, especially in and on the home. Personalize the palette by including an accent of an unconventional color, like a toned-down teal.

RED

YELLOW

GREEN

BLUE

VIOLET

PINK

ORANGE
& BROWN

NEUTRAL

GRAY

New Neutrals

As beige and gray duke it out over the position of top neutral, consider other less common neutrals as alternatives. Shades of brown get a fresh twist with undertones of yellow and green. Navy blues can step up and fill in for black.

RED

YELLOW

GREEN

BLUE

VIOLET

PINK

ORANGE
& BROWN

NEUTRAL

GRAY

Cool with Brown and Blue

Blue and orange are complementary colors, opposite each other on the color wheel. When used together they form a lively, dynamic color scheme. Tone down the energy level a notch by swapping orange for its more toned-down relation, brown.

RED
YELLOW
GREEN
BLUE
VIOLET
PINK
ORANGE & BROWN
NEUTRAL
GRAY

gray

A Few Shades of Gray

Monochromatic palettes have an air of quiet elegance, especially when the shades range from white to black. Play around with the gray a bit and use warm and cool shades together. This keeps the palette from feeling dreary or dull.

RED

YELLOW

GREEN

BLUE

VIOLET

PINK

ORANGE
& BROWN

NEUTRAL

GRAY

Warmly Gray

Take the heavy edge off black and dark brown hues with a generous helping of a warm gray. This handsome scheme has a high-end vibe, especially with the addition of glimmering gold elements and details.

RED
YELLOW
GREEN
BLUE
VIOLET
PINK
ORANGE & BROWN
NEUTRAL
GRAY

Neutral Mix

Neither too hot nor too cold, this color scheme gets it just right. Gather an assortment of warm and cool grays, and then add contrast with black and white. Tie it all together with a delectable dash of caramel.

RED

YELLOW

GREEN

BLUE

VIOLET

PINK

ORANGE
& BROWN

NEUTRAL

GRAY

Spiced Gray

Add a squirt of spicy orange to an assortment of grays for a pleasing blend of warm and cool colors. A cooler blue-gray provides a contrasting foil to orange, whereas a neutral or warm gray offers a more harmonious vibe.

RED

YELLOW

GREEN

BLUE

VIOLET

PINK

ORANGE
& BROWN

NEUTRAL

GRAY

Hot and Cool

Shimmery silver gray looks hot when paired with deep, lush reds. Play up the drama with generous amounts of black and red. Or, for a palette that has more of a quiet appeal, up the amount of white and gray and limit the darker hues to accents only.

RED

YELLOW

GREEN

BLUE

VIOLET

PINK

ORANGE
& BROWN

NEUTRAL

GRAY

Go for Gold

It's common to pair golden yellows with red, orange or brown — fellow warm hues. Break with tradition and use them with gray instead. A yellow and cool gray scheme will have a dynamic quality, whereas a warm gray pairing will feel more relaxed.

RED
YELLOW
GREEN
BLUE
VIOLET
PINK
ORANGE
& BROWN
NEUTRAL
GRAY

Exquisite Emerald

We tend to associate dark green shades with trees deep in the forest. But, instead of pairing these greens with wood-like, bark-brown hues, shake things up and add soft gray instead. It's a surprising combination with a youthful and modern feel.

RED

YELLOW

GREEN

BLUE

VIOLET

PINK

ORANGE
& BROWN

NEUTRAL

GRAY

Aqua Accent

Give a gray color scheme a tropical kick with the addition of aqua. Aqua and turquoise are blue hues that have a touch of yellow in them. This warms them up slightly and prevents the palette from feeling frosty.

RED

YELLOW

GREEN

BLUE

VIOLET

PINK

ORANGE
& BROWN

NEUTRAL

GRAY

Cool with the Blues

Medium to dark blue-grays are a fantastic alternative to basic black in a color scheme. Where black can go a bit stern, stuffy or flat, these blue-gray hues offer a softer option. Keep it cool with additions of crisp cobalt and inky indigo.

RED

YELLOW

GREEN

BLUE

VIOLET

PINK

ORANGE & BROWN

NEUTRAL

GRAY

Proud as a Peacock

Gray hues are an excellent choice for the base or background layer in a color scheme. To this neutral foundation you can layer in bright and boisterous color, such as a bold and beautiful peacock blue.

RED
YELLOW
GREEN
BLUE
VIOLET
PINK
ORANGE & BROWN
NEUTRAL
GRAY

Flirting with Gray

For a sophisticated take on sweet pastels, select hues that have a touch of gray in them instead of just white. This gives the colors a muted and neutral quality. The complex character of these tones allows them to be used in a variety of schemes.

RED
YELLOW
GREEN
BLUE
VIOLET
PINK
ORANGE & BROWN
NEUTRAL
GRAY

Wink of Pink

This delightful palette of cool blue-grays with a selection of soft pinks is a flirty marriage of color. It's elegant without being too stuffy or serious. Use it for spaces and occasions when a polished, yet fun vibe is what you're after.

RED

YELLOW

GREEN

BLUE

VIOLET

PINK

ORANGE
& BROWN

NEUTRAL

GRAY

Gray Gardens

Many people shy away from gray because they consider it to be a cold, stark and uninviting color. Here's a gray scheme that is happy, fun and party-ready. Flirty, fruity hues add just enough zest and energy to keep everyone in light spirits.

RED

YELLOW

GREEN

BLUE

VIOLET

PINK

ORANGE
& BROWN

NEUTRAL

GRAY

Index

A
analogous colors 15, 154, 182
autumn 34, 68, 162
  Autumnal Orange 206–207

B
black 15
  A Few Shades of Gray 260–261
  A Splash of Magenta 172–173
  Black, White and Red All Over 18–19
  Blue is the New Black 112–113
  Burnished Bronze 216–217
  Cool with Yellow 60–61
  Hot and Cool 268–269
  Khaki Contrast 228–229
  Mellow Yellow 62–63
  Neutral Mix 264–265
  New Neutrals 254–255
  Opposites Attract 26–27
  Orange Drama 204–205
  Real Red 40–41
  Warmly Gray 262–263
blue
  Aqua Accent 274–275
  Blue Chip 110–111
  Blue is the New Black 112–113
  Blue Print 138–139
  Blue Ribbon 108–109
  Bold Complements of Blue 114–115
  Cool and Sunny 132–133
  Cool Blue 210–211
  Cool with Brown and Blue 256–257
  Cool with the Blues 276–277
  Coolly Exotic 122–123
  Go Navy 134–135
  Icy Blue 136–137
  Into the Blue 126–127
  New Neutrals 254–255
  New Patriot 118–119
  Not Your Baby's Blue 120–121
  Out of the Blue 116–117
  Proud as a Peacock 278–279
  Taking the Waters 128–129
  Teal Tease 140–141
  Tonal Teal 252–253
  Tropical Aqua 130–131
  Under a Clear Blue Sky 124–125
brown
  Brown Butterscotch 242–243
  Burnished Bronze 216–217
  Coffee and Cream 222–223
  Cool Blue 210–211
  Cool with Brown and Blue 256–257
  Dark and Decadent 224–225
  Down to Earth 214–215
  Dulce de Leche 212–213
  Golden Glow 208–209
  Sisal and Soft Pink 220–221
  Warm Shimmer 218–219

C
chroma 15, 120, 192
color combinations 12–15
color wheel 14–15
complementary colors 14–15, 22, 26, 74,
  148, 166, 210, 256
  Bold Complements of Blue 114–115
  Colorful Complements 22–23
  near complementary colors 52, 104, 158,
    162
  Opposites Attract 26–27
cool colors 15, 56, 84, 102, 136, 140, 158,
  202, 216, 218, 232, 236, 244, 260, 264, 266,
  270, 282
  Cool and Sunny 132–133
  Cool Blue 210–211

Cool Violet 154–155
Cool with Brown and Blue 256–257
Cool with Green 102–103
Cool with the Blues 276–277
Cool with Yellow 60–61
Coolly Exotic 122–123
Coolly Purple 146–147
Hot and Cool 268–269
Hot Pink and Cool Purple 170–171
Red Hot Meets Cool Gray 24–25
contrast 15, 26, 74, 104, 114, 122, 162, 168,
  174, 204, 244, 264, 266

F
fall *see* autumn

G
gold 104, 262
  Blue Chip 110–111
  Bold Red and Gold 30–31
  Bold with Gold 68–69
  Evergreen 92–93
  Go for Gold 270–271
  Golden Glow 208–209
  Golden Harvest 66–67
gray
  A Few Shades of Gray 260–261
  Aqua Accent 274–275
  Cool with the Blues 276–277
  Exquisite Emerald 272–273
  Flirting with Gray 280–281
  Glamorous with Gray 150–151
  Go for Gold 270–271
  Gray Gardens 284–285
  Hot and Cool 268–269
  Neutral Mix 264–265
  Orange Drama 204–205
  Proud as a Peacock 278–279
  Red Hot Meets Cool Gray 24–25
  Spiced Gray 266–267
  Warmly Gray 262–263
  Wink of Pink 282–283
green
  Bordering on Blueberry 160–161
  Colorful Complements 22–23
  Cool with Green 102–103
  Coral and Sea Glass 248–249
  Cream with Deep Green 244–245
  Darkly Sage 84–85
  Emerald Elegance 94–95
  Enviably Green 72–73
  Evergreen 92–93
  Evergreen and Cranberry 96–97
  Exquisite Emerald 272–273
  Grassy Green 90–91
  Green with a Pop of Preppy Pink 74–75
  Miami Mix 100–101
  Modern Green 80–81
  Mushroom and Moss 238–239
  Muted Mint 86–87
  Neutral Greens 88–89
  Peacock Greens 78–79
  Petal Pink on Stem Green 166–167
  Pink with Frosty Green 174–175
  Rainy Day Greens 82–83
  Soft with Celery 240–241
  Sublime 76–77
  Teal Appeal 104–105
  Violet with Aqua Greens 158–159

M
modern palettes 24, 28, 64, 140, 150, 218,
  232, 272
  Modern Green 80–81
  Modern Orange 202–203
monochromatic palettes 208, 236, 260

N
neutrals
  A Better Beige 232–233
  Berries and Chocolate 250–251
  Brown Butterscotch 242–243
  Cinnamon Spice 230–231
  Cool with Brown and Blue 256–257
  Coral and Sea Glass 248–249
  Cream with Deep Green 244–245
  Khaki Contrast 228–229
  Mushroom and Moss 238–239
  Neutral Greens 88–89
  Neutral Mix 264–265
  New Neutrals 254–255
  Red with Warm Neutrals 28–29
  Russet Roundup 234–235
  Soft with Celery 240–241
  Tobacco and Camel 246–247
  Tonal Teal 252–253
  Wicker and Wood 236–237

O
orange
  Autumnal Orange 206–207
  Bold Complements of Blue 114–115
  Cool Blue 210–211
  Modern Orange 202–203
  Orange Drama 204–205
  Orange Sherbet 200–201
  Orange Spice 192–193
  Outgoing Orange 194–195
  Playful Citrus 196–197
  Summertime Orange 198–199

P
paint blending 14
pastels 176, 124, 280
peach
  Just Peachy 182–183
pink
  A Splash of Magenta 172–173
  Blush of Pink 180–181
  Deep yet Rosy 184–185
  Hot Pink and Cool Purple 170–171
  Just Peachy 182–183
  Moving Toward Mauve 186–187
  Petal Pink on Stem Green 166–167
  Pink with Frosty Green 174–175
  Playfully Pink 168–169
  Sisal and Soft Pink 220–221
  Summertime Pinks 178–179
  Think Spring Pink 176–177
  Wink of Pink 282–283
primary colors 14, 15
purple
  Coolly Purple 146–147
  Hot Pink and Cool Purple 170–171
  Purple Paired with Garnet 164–165

R
red
  Berries and Chocolate 250–251
  Black, White and Red All Over 18–19
  Bold Red and Gold 30–31
  Cheery Cherry and Violet 148–149
  Colorful Complements 22–23
  Dark and Decadent 224–225
  Evergreen and Cranberry 96–97
  Hint of Red 42–43
  Hot and Cool 268–269
  Juicy Reds 38–39
  Opposites Attract 26–27
  Real Red 40–41
  Red Blush 44–45
  Red Hot Meets Cool Gray 24–25
  Red with Warm Neutrals 28–29

Red Zest 20–21
Rich with Reds 32–33
Tawny Tones 34–35
Top of the Rainbow 36–37

S
saturation 15
  de-saturated colors 42, 100
  highly saturated colors 40, 160, 234
  saturated colors 80, 92, 96, 170
secondary colors 14, 15
shades 15, 42, 118, 120, 168, 204, 210, 212,
  232, 234, 254, 260, 272
sophisticated palettes 24, 32, 170, 224, 280
spring 38, 124, 198
  Think Spring Pink 176–177
summer 52, 100, 132
  Midsummer Yellow 56–57
  Summer Sunflower 48–49
  Summertime Orange 198–199
  Summertime Pinks 178–179

T
tertiary colors 14, 15
tints 15, 42, 54, 176, 204, 212
tones 15, 42, 120, 134, 212, 216, 230, 280
  toned-down colors 28, 34, 88, 118, 162,
    168, 184, 186, 196, 198, 210, 234, 252, 256
triadic colors 168
tropical palettes 72, 274
  Tropical Aqua 130–131

U
undertones 34, 58, 64, 84, 98, 130, 140, 160,
  214, 240, 244, 254,

V
values 15, 176, 192, 240
violet
  Bordering on Blueberry 160–161
  Cheery Cherry and Violet 148–149
  Cool Violet 154–155
  Coolly Purple 146–147
  Glamorous with Gray 150–151
  Grape Harvest 162–163
  Lilac and Lavender 156–157
  Purple Paired with Garnet 164–165
  Rich Eggplant 152–153
  Violet Forest 144–145
  Violet with Aqua Greens 158–159

W
warm colors 15, 20, 40, 66, 68, 94, 108, 134,
  146, 152, 178, 186, 194, 202, 206, 208, 216,
  230, 234, 236, 244, 252, 260, 266, 270, 274
  Red with Warm Neutrals 28–29
  Warm Shimmer 218–219
  Warmly Gray 262–263
white
  Black, White, and Red All Over 18–19

Y
yellow
  Bold with Gold 68–69
  Citrus Zest 50–51
  Cool with Yellow 60–61
  Golden Harvest 66–67
  Lemon Chiffon 54–55
  Lemonade 58–59
  Mellow Yellow 62–63
  Midsummer Yellow 56–57
  Serious Yellow 64–65
  Summer Sunflower 48–49
  The Sun in the Sky 52–53
youthful palettes 26, 90, 140, 170, 178, 272

Credits

Images for each page are credited clockwise from top left. All images listed in italics have come from **Shutterstock.com**. While every effort has been made to credit contributors, Quarto would like to apologize should there have been any errors or omissions — and would be pleased to make the appropriate correction for future editions of the book.

p. 2 Abode, Living4media.co.uk; *SJ Travel Photo and Video; SvetlanaSF;* The Contemporary Home, Tch.net; *Sam Aronov;* Henri Del Olmo, Living4media.co.uk; *emin kuliyev; wernerimages; Manamana*
p. 18 *Jalag / Olaf Szczepaniak,* Living4media.co.uk
p. 19 *Alik Mulikov; Maria Sbytova; TatyanaMH; Viktoria Minkova; lemony; lancelot; Sergey Causelove*
p. 20 *photoff*
p. 21 *Ekaterina Pokrovsky; L.F; Elena Elisseeva; Caroline Guest; inomasa; Lodimup; Mihail Jershov*
p. 22 *Anatoliy Cherkas*
p. 23 *Xanya69; Sergey Melnikov; Gina Smith;* Steven Morris, Living4media.co.uk; *biggunsband;* Joshua Resnick
p. 24 Lars Ranek, Living4media.co.uk
p. 25 *Jolanta Beinarovica;* Henri Del Olmo, Living4media. co.uk; *Ondacaracola; claudiodivizia; Kichigin; 3523studio; freya-photographer*
p. 26 *mubus7*
p. 27 *Photographee.eu; tomertu;* Ovidiu Hrubaru; *sorayafaii; Augustino; Ruth Black*
p. 28 *kqlsm*
p. 29 *MJTH; Joshua Rainey Photography; Tatyana Tomsickova; Catalin Petolea;* 1000 Words; *VitaliY_Kharin_ and_Maya; filmlandscape*
p. 30 Ruth Black
p. 31 *Esat Photography;* Abode, Living4media.co.uk; *Andrey Sarymsakov; prapann; rawmn*
p. 32 *Viktoria Minkova*
p. 33 *sanneberg; FashionStock.com; Douglas Sherman; YSK1;* Great Stock!, Living4media.co.uk; *v.s.anandhakrishna; Evgenialevi*
p. 34 Radoslaw Wojnar, Living4media.co.uk; *daylightistanbul studio*
p. 35 *Miro Vrlik Photography; Jo Green; Nejron Photo; Greg Henry; lightecho; Agnes Kantaruk;* Steven Morris, Living4media.co.uk
p. 36 *Capture Light*
p. 37 *A_Lesik; Ruth Black; blackboard1965; iravgustin; Roman Podvysotskiy; Letterberry*
p. 38 Abode, Living4media.co.uk
p. 39 *Alex Gukalov; Evgeniya Porechenskaya; webwaffe; Dasha Petrenko; Felix Britanski; Martin Mecnarowski*
p. 40 *lancelot; Roman Sigaev*
p. 41 *Africa Studio;* Yassen Hristov, Living4media.co.uk; *Shana Schnur; Neale Cousland; Daniela Pelazza; Nishihama; Alex Halay*
p. 42 *Irene Barajas; Bronwyn Photo*
p. 43 *Sveta Yaroshuk; Naphat_Jorjee; Vladimir Khirman; Natalia Klenova; Dmitry Abaza; conejota; Volodymyr Leshchenko*
p. 44 *Breadmaker*
p. 45 Frank Sanchez, Living4media.co.uk; *Ruta Production; Bas Meelker; Katsiaryna Yudo; Andre van der Veen; Dmitry Zubarev*
p. 48 *SJ Travel Photo and Video*
p. 49 *Selenit; Dejan Lazarevic; Photographee.eu; Vadim Zholobov;* Caroline Guest; *gradi1975; 24Novembers*
p. 50 *FashionStock.com; Africa Studio*
p. 51 *Sophie McAulay; Chris Curtis; aastock; Maria Sbytova; Ruth Black;* Paul Ryan-Goff, Living4media.co.uk
p. 52 *chrishumphreys*
p. 53 *Laitr Keiows; biggunsband; Alexander Image; hofhauser; biggunsband; photo_master2000; Iriana Shiyan*
p. 54 *Dean Pennala*
p. 55 *Dmitry Abaza; Marcel Jancovic; trgowanlock; blackboard1965;* Bratt Décor, brattdecor.com; *zagorodnaya;* Joshua Rainey Photography; *Africa Studio*
p. 56 *Kamira*
p. 57 *Aleshyn_Andrei; Juli Scalzi; Andrekart Photography;* 1000 Words; *nioloxs;* Abode, Living4media.co.uk; *IS_ImageSource,* istockphoto.com; *Daniela Pelazza*

p. 58 *Alex Gukalov*
p. 59 *kuzsvetlaya; Alex Gukalov; kregeg; Alex Gukalov; Andrew McDonough; zadirako; milosljubicic; luanateutzi*
p. 60 Steven Morris, Living4media.co.uk
p. 61 *Dmitry_Tsvetkov; Maria Sbytova; Photographee.eu;* Ovidiu Hrubaru; *daylightistanbul studio; aastock; Maria Sbytova; fabiodevilla*
p. 62 *Stefano Tinti*
p. 63 *ArTono; Photographee.eu; Essential Image Media; ball2be; FashionStock.com;* View Pictures, Living4media.co. uk; *iordani*
p. 64 *FashionStock.com; lancelot*
p. 65 *Karkas; Neirfy; karamysh; WorldWide; Chawalit S; Chris15232*
p. 66 *lancelot*
p. 67 *Joshua Rainey Photography; Gianni Sala,* Living4media. co.uk; *EpicStockMedia; Gary Yim; Iriana Shiyan; hxdbzxy; Olga Lipatova*
p. 68 *Vincent St. Thomas; Vladimir Melnik*
p. 69 *FashionStock.com;* Caroline Guest; *SunKids; andershprono; Maxim Kostenko;* BRABBU, brabbu.com
p. 72 *Butterfly Hunter*
p. 73 *Goran Bogicevic; kpatyhka;* Nina Struve, Living4media. co.uk; *c12; Tatyana Borodina; Patryk Kosmider*
p. 74 *TOMO; Tr1sha*
p. 75 *Oleh_Slobodeniuk,* istockphoto.com; Pics On-Line / June Tuesday, Living4media.co.uk; *jesadaphorn; Olga Popkova; Leena Robinson; Anna Ismagilova; Natalia Kirichenko*
p. 76 Abode, Living4media.co.uk
p. 77 *Maria Sbytova; FashionStock.com; hlphoto; PS Prometheus; vitals; Pavel Vakhrushev; liatris; Andrey Sarymsakov*
p. 78 *Viktoriia Chursina*
p. 79 *Jalag / Olaf Szczepaniak,* Living4media.co.uk; *Eco Chic,* ecochic.com.au; *ChameleonsEye; Anna Ismagilova; SvetlanaSF; Artur Synenko; Shana Schnur*
p. 80 *mazur serhiy; Hank Shiffman*
p. 81 *Andreas G. Karelias;* Graham & Brown, Grahambrown. com; *florinstana; Nattle; Chananchida Ch;* Great Stock!, Living4media.co.uk; *Shutterstock.com; Africa Studio*
p. 82 Great Stock!, Living4media.co.uk
p. 83 Ovidiu Hrubaru; *daisydaisy;* Annette & Christian, Living4media.co.uk; *s_karau; sootra; Alina Galieva; Photographee.eu*
p. 84 Graham & Brown, Grahambrown.com; *Maria Sbytova*
p. 85 *Masson; Brando Cimarosti,* Living4media.co.uk; *George Koultouridis; Jacques PALUT; Makela Mona; dfrolovXIII*
p. 86 *MJTH*
p. 87 *Shutterstock.com; Pablo Scapinachis; Iriana Shiyan; Catwalk Photos; Karen Grigoryan; Julia Karo*
p. 88 *pics721*
p. 89 *chrishumphreys; artesiawells; Your Inspiration;* Winfried Heinze, Living4media.co.uk; *Musing Tree Design; Shana Schnur; Kurkul; Rebecca Dickerson*
p. 90 Great Stock!, Living4media.co.uk; *fjphoto*
p. 91 *aastock; Champiofoto; Camille White; Kira Vasilevski; Roman Zhuk; Alex Gukalov*
p. 92 Per Magnus Persson, Living4media.co.uk
p. 93 *Dasha Petrenko; Nata Sha; Halfpoint; ShortPhotos; Dimitrios; Oleksii Nykonchuk;* View Pictures, Living4media. co.uk; *lazyllama*
p. 94 Yassen Hristov, Living4media.co.uk
p. 95 *aastock; adpePhoto; Aleshyn_Andrei; Sam Aronov; eelnosiva; Alex Gukalov; Evgeniya Porechenskaya*
p. 96 *KellyNelson*
p. 97 *Karen Grigoryan; Eva Tigrova; Natalya Osipova;* Paul Ryan-Goff, Living4media.co.uk; *Undivided*
p. 98 Sanderson, Sanderson.co.uk
p. 99 *Jovana Veljkovic; Goran Bogicevic; SJ Allen; Paul Prescott; Difeng Zhu; Evgeny Atamanenko*

p. 100 *Mickrick,* istockphoto.com
p. 101 *Litvinov; Jacek_Kadaj; MR.LIGHTMAN1975;* Andreas von Einsiedel, Living4media.co.uk; *FashionStock.com;* Dash & Albert; *Alexander Demyanenko*
p. 102 Great Stock!, Living4media.co.uk; *Dark Moon Pictures*
p. 103 *Sam Aronov; SOMKKU; PAUL ATKINSON; FashionStock.com;* Radoslaw Wojnar; *578foot*
p. 104 *Yulia Grigoryeva*
p. 105 *Nata Sha; stockphoto mania; Alla Simacheva; photoagent; lancelot; Milkos*
p. 108 *Evgeniya Porechenskaya*
p. 109 *Andreea Cracium; Evgeniya Porechenskaya; Alex Halay;* Ann Haritonenko; Abode, Living4media.co.uk
p. 110 View Pictures, Living4media.co.uk
p. 111 *Andrey Valerevich Kiselev; Matthew Ennis; Sophie McAulay; Fuyu Liu; Maria Sbytova;* MiaFleur- online homewares, Miafleur.com; *Michael C. Gray;* The Contemporary Home, Tch.net
p. 112 *KUPRYNENKO ANDRII*
p. 113 Ranek, Lars, Living4media.co.uk; *Alexandru Matusciac; PlusONE; MARCHPN; JuliyaNorenko; WorldWide*
p. 114 *filil*
p. 115 *Photographee.eu; Sidhe;* Ovidiu Hrubaru; *aprilante; imagIN.gr photography; Brum; Chantal de Bruijne*
p. 116 *siculodoc,* iStockphoto.com
p. 117 *Steven Coling; SvetlanaSF; Neale Cousland; StevenRussellSmithPhotos; Evgeniya Porechenskaya;* Jeremy Levine Design, Jeremylevine.com/Flickr The Commons
p. 118 Radoslaw Wojnar, Living4media.co.uk
p. 119 *Lecyk Radoslaw; FashionStock.com; Karniewska; matthewnigel; Stefano Tinti; PlusONE*
p. 120 *Tr1sha*
p. 121 *irbis pictures;* Radoslaw Wojnar, Living4media.co.uk; *leonori; catwalker; Agnes Kantaruk; WorldWide;* Graham & Brown, Grahambrown.com
p. 122 *Stefano Tinti*
p. 123 *Envyligh; Jiri Vaclavek;* Sarah Hogan, Living4media. co.uk; *Maryna Kopylova;* Radoslaw Wojnar, Living4media.co. uk; *infinity21; Jeannette Katzir Photog*
p. 124 *Deborah Kolb*
p. 125 *vinogradnaya;* Ovidiu Hrubaru; *Prasit Rodphan; Ruth Black; MorganStudio; Prasit Rodphan; MorganStudio*
p. 126 Annette & Christian, Living4media.co.uk; *Christian Bertrand*
p. 127 *Robynrg; Julianna; sirirak kaewgorn; marinomarini; Ruth Black; elitravo*
p. 128 Stuart Cox, Living4media.co.uk; *mates*
p. 129 *InnaFelker; Frolova_Elena; elitravo; Meg Wallace Photography; Ecaterina Petrova; lizabarbiza; Lucy Liu*
p. 130 *Kati Molin*
p. 131 *gephoto; Galina Tcivina; Anna Oleksenko; FashionStock.com; Ecaterina Petrova; Kagual; Elina Leonova*
p. 132 *MillaF*
p. 133 *Jalag / Veronika Stark,* Living4media.co.uk; *HighKey; Pabkov; Victoria Minkova; Ruth Black; arustamova; Anna Antonova; Capture Light*
p. 134 Tara Striano, Living4media.co.uk
p. 135 *sakhorn; Zheng HUANG; Arina P. Habich; Dragon Images; Chris15232; evgeny freeone; AGITA LEIMANE*
p. 136 *WorldWide;* Martin Kudrjavcev
p. 137 Stefan Thurmann, Living4media.co.uk; *conrado;* Idyll Home, Idyllhome.co.uk; *FashionStock.com; B. and E. Dudzinscy;* Robert Varga
p. 138 *Goran Bogicevic*
p. 139 Inge Ofenstein, Living4media.co.uk; *asharkyu; Stefano Tinti; Angela Luchianiuc; Guy Erwood; Dyo;* Winfried Heinze, Living4media.co.uk; *Vikmanis Ints*
p. 140 Mentis Photography, Inc., Living4media.co.uk
p. 141 BRABBU, brabbu.com; *Vladzimirska Svyatoslava;* View Pictures, Living4media.co.uk; *Chris15232; Only Fabrizio; blakeley; Percold*
p. 144 *eelnosiva*
p. 145 *wandee007;* Anne Kitzman; *ariadna de raadt; FashionStock.com; kai keisuke; Yana Godenko; Tom Tom; Igors Rusakovs*
p. 146 *Alex Gukalov*

p. 147 *Elena Rostunova; Abode, Living4media.co.uk; Ruslan Iefremov; Tom Lester; crystalfoto; Discovod; Miro Vrlik Photography; Castka; KOBRIN PHOTO*
p. 148 *KPG_Payless; totojang1977*
p. 149 *Belovodchenko Anton; piccaya; Joshua Rainey Photography; Andrea Haase; Henri Del Olmo, Living4media. co.uk; Africa Studio; Maria Sbytova; Eve81*
p. 150 *lancelot*
p. 151 *FashionStock.com; Magdanatka; wernerimages; FashionStock.com; Illya Vinogradov; irbis pictures; ChameleonsEye*
p. 152 *Simon Maxwell Photography, Living4media.co.uk; Petar Djordjevic*
p. 153 *Tapetenfabrik Gebr. Rasch GmbH & Co. KG, rasch-tapete.de; Ausf; Deatonphotos; Africa Studio; Sam Aronov; tymonko; Tom Lester*
p. 154 *AdrianC*
p. 155 *Phatthanit; Dmitry Abaza; Elena Rostunova; melis; Jayne Chapman; Annette & Christian, Living4media.co.uk; maryloeo; PonomarenkoNataly*
p. 156 Bärbel Miebach, Living4media.co.uk
p. 157 *IVASHstudio; TorriPhoto; Ovidiu Hrubaru; Tr1sha; Wichudapa; Champiofoto; Juta*
p. 158 *Alla Simacheva; Massel_Marina*
p. 159 *FashionStock.com; locrifa; StacieStaufffSmith Photos; JMS Splash Photography; Oksana Shufrych; smartape; Evgheni Lachi; WorldWide*
p. 160 *Shebeko*
p. 161 *dragi52; Shebeko; Shebeko; A_Lesik; Seqoya; Dobermaraner; Oleksandr Lipko*
p. 162 *Michael Warwick*
p. 163 *Jakkrit Orrasri; Kachergina; Karin Jaehne; matthewnigel; TorriPhoto; Still AB*
p. 164 *Evangelos Paterakis, Living4media.co.uk; maoyunping*
p. 165 *Yana Godenko; Mariya Volik; Ovidiu Hrubaru; Melica; Sergio Stakhnyk; Carpet Vista, Coloured Vintage and Nepal Original, CarpetVista.com; rehanq*
p. 168 *Natalia Van Doninck*
p. 169 *Paul Matthew Photography; Lucy Liu; Joshua Rainey Photography; IBL Bildbyra AB / Angelica, Söderberg, Living4media.co.uk; Asaf Eliason; AppStock; tanger*
p. 170 *Neale Cousland*
p. 171 *Evgeniy Porechenskaya; Everything; NinaMalyna; Cecilia Möller, Living4media.co.uk; Ecaterina Petrova; WeStudio*
p. 172 *Cecilia Möller, Living4media.co.uk*
p. 173 *locrifa; Evgeniya Porechenskaya; Gina Smith; elitravo; popovartem.com; Lim Yong Hian; Tarzhanova; emin kuliyev*
p. 174 *Yassen Hristov*
p. 175 *Ovidiu Hrubaru; Ruth Black; Forewer; wandee007; D_D; Victoria Minkova; aastock*
p. 176 *Ruth Black; Marilyn Barbone*
p. 177 Syl Loves, Living4media.co.uk; *akayuki; Alena Ozerova; All About Space; Ruth Black;* Tom Meadow, Living4media.co.uk; *Kaspars Grinvalds*
p. 178 *Odrida*
p. 179 *Anna-Mari West; FXQuadro; CLS Design; Det-anan; Andrekart Photography;* Syl Loves, Living4media.co.uk; *Ruth Black*
p. 180 *Ruth Black; Paul Rich Studio*
p. 181 *danielo; Agnes Kantaruk; AS Inc; IBL Bildbyra AB / Peter Ericsson, Living4media.co.uk; Andrii Kobryn; Ruth Black*
p. 182 Annette & Christian, Living4media.co.uk; *Shell114*
p. 183 Art Hide - Stylist Tess Beagley and Photographer Carrie Young, Arthide.co; *Fotokon; Maria Iial; cameilia;* iDecorate; idecorateshop.com; *carlo dapino; Beto Chagas*
p. 184 *kazoka*
p. 185 *Ovidiu Hrubaru; Photographee.eu; MiaFleur- online homewares. Styling and photography: Amelia and Jacqui Brooks, Miafleur.com; Magdanatka; Vladislav Plotnikov; Oleg Elena Tovkach; vinogradnaya*
p. 186 *Yana Godenko; Wig*
p. 187 *Miro Vrlik Photography; Robert Fesus; Vitalii Tiagunov; Evgeniya Porechenskaya; elitravo; kostrez; Sergey Chirkov*
p. 188 *Robert Varga*
p. 189 *FashionStock.com; SATHIANPONG PHOOKIT; John Copland; Dmitry Abaza; OmiStudio; Hteam; vinogradnaya*
p. 192 *Chris15232*
p. 193 *FashionStock.com; Andrey Kucheruk; Karen Grigoryan;* Bärbel Miebach, Living4media.co.uk; *Niradj; TOMO*
p. 194 *anat chant*
p. 195 *bostonphotographer; David Tadevosian; Patrick Foto; Manamana; Masson; Nata Sha; Debbi Gerdt; photobyjoy*

p. 196 Annette & Christian, Living4media.co.uk
p. 197 *Lifebrary; Goran Bogicevic; FashionStock.com; c12; Alex Andrei; aastock*
p. 198 Bratt Décor, brattdecor.com
p. 199 *Jodie Johnson; goldenjack; Yuriy Kuzakov; Henrique Daniel Araujo; aastock; Ovidiu Hrubaru*
p. 200 *catwalker*
p. 201 *Rade Kovac; Gianni Sala, Living4media.co.uk; Anastasiia Kryvenok; Nadya Korobkova; Alexander Tihonov; Alinute Silzeviciute*
p. 202 Annette & Christian, Living4media.co.uk
p. 203 *Breadmaker; Alexandru Matusciac; 3523studio; Chris15232; Ruth Black; Oleksandr Rostov*
p. 204 *Tapetenfabrik Gebr. Rasch GmbH & Co. KG, rasch-tapete.de*
p. 205 *aastock; Wayne Vincent, Living4media.co.uk; Robsonphoto; taniavolobueva; Dmitry Abaza; Neale Cousland; kees luiten*
p. 206 *Maleo*
p. 207 *Eric Limon; Shana Schnur; Ashwin; Andrey Armyagov; Winfried Heinze, Living4media.co.uk; Alexandre Zveiger*
p. 208 *Rene van der Hulst, Living4media.co.uk*
p. 209 *aastock; Rogndano Srdanovic; Anastasiia Kryvenok; FashionStock.com; KULISH VIKTORIIA; Ann Haritonenko; Everything*
p. 210 *polusvet; IVASHstudio*
p. 211 *Max Smolyar; Lukasz Zandecki, Living4media.co.uk; MIKHAIL MAKOVKIN; Ulrika Ekblom, Living4media.co.uk; VOJTa Herout; c12*
p. 212 Simon Scarboro, Living4media.co.uk
p. 213 *Arina P. Habich; Photographee.eu; Karen Grigoryan; Guas; Marion Abada; nico99*
p. 214 *aprilante*
p. 215 *Wayne Vincent, Living4media.co.uk; Superlime; Natalia Priadilshchikova; bezikus; kregeg; L.F*
p. 216 Radoslaw Wojnar, Living4media.co.uk
p. 217 *Sufi; Volodymyr Shulevskyy; Alexandre Zveiger; Photographee.eu; Aleshyn_Andrei; Shutterstock.com*
p. 218 *Alexandre Zveiger*
p. 219 *Miro Vrlik Photography; Alexandre Zveiger; IVASHstudio; Ruth Black; Victoria_Fox;* View Pictures, Living4media.co.uk
p. 220 *Great Stock!, Living4media.co.uk*
p. 221 *Kaspars Grinvalds; Kateryna Mostova; Syda Productions; arustamova; Tr1sha; Gordana Sermek; StrelaStudio*
p. 222 *Branko Jovanovic*
p. 223 Jalag / Angelika Lorenzen, Living4media.co.uk; *Ovidiu Hrubaru; paultarasenko; Tata Mamai; WorldWide; 5 second Studio*
p. 224 *Luci italiane. Evi Style by Stefano Mandruzzato, Luciitaliane.com; Irina Tischenko*
p. 225 *indira's work; Alexandre Zveiger; Diego Schtutman; ThitareeS; Svetlana Lukienko; Wiratchai wansamngam*
p. 228 Annette & Christian, Living4media.co.uk
p. 229 *bikeriderlondon; aprilante; Ovidiu Hrubaru; Maglara; Eric Limon; Chantal de Bruijne*
p. 230 *LarisaS*
p. 231 *Miro Vrlik Photography; sl_photo; Maria Sbytova; Sisacorn; lkpro; Anna Subbotina; plepraisaeng; Melanie Hobson*
p. 232 *Santiago Cornejo*
p. 233 *KUPRYNENKO ANDRII; michaeljung; eelnosiva; Alex Gukalov; Ulyana Khorunzha; lev radin; Faiz Zaki*
p. 234 View Pictures, Living4media.co.uk
p. 235 *blueeyes; Ann Haritonenko; MNStudio; Ana Photo; attila; eelnosiva*
p. 236 Lukasz Zandecki, Living4media.co.uk
p. 237 *Caroline Guest; triocean; Agnes Kantaruk; USAart studio; Dmitry Abaza; Joshua Rainey Photography; Anastasiia Kryvenok*
p. 238 *Ingrid Maasik*
p. 239 *Alexandre Zveiger; Gerasia; Yuliya Yafimik; Sussie Bell, Living4media.co.uk; Iriana Shiyan; Lucy Baldwin*
p. 240 *piccaya; avers*
p. 241 *Sanderson, Sanderson-uk.com; FashionStock.com; Alberto P; Photo Africa; Tr1sha; Graham & Brown, Grahambrown.com*
p. 242 Bernard Touillon, Living4media.co.uk
p. 243 *Kartinkin77; Olga Lipatova; Vladzimirska Svyatoslava; Jay Petersen; ShortPhotos; bikeriderlondon*
p. 244 *All About Space; Alex Gukalov*
p. 245 *Kagual;* Brando Cimarosti, Living4media.co.uk; *Stefano Tronci; Aleksie; Kenneth Keifer; Mathe, Dorottya; JuliyaNorenko*

p. 246 Rachael Smith, Living4media.co.uk
p. 247 *design.at.krooogle; FashionStock.com; WorldWide; Karen Grigoran; WorldWide; BRABBU, brabbu.com*
p. 248 *Alex Gukalov*
p. 249 *kuvona; Anatoliy Cherkas; Great Stock!, Living4media. co.uk; Alex Gukalov; Sophie McAulay; Ovidiu Hrubaru; syrotkin; Marilyn Barbone*
p. 250 Guy Bouchet, Living4media.co.uk
p. 251 *IVASHstudio; Nikolas_jkd; Santiago Cornejo; Viktoriia Chursina; zhekoss; Owl_photographer; Studio ART; Bogdan Sonjachnyj*
p. 252 Rachael Smith, Living4media.co.uk
p. 253 IN-SPACES, In-spaces.com; *Radoslaw Lecyk; pongnathee kluaythong; Andrekart Photography; Photographee.eu; brodtcast; Sam Aronov*
p. 254 *Great Stock!, Living4media.co.uk*
p. 255 *KUPRYNENKO ANDRII; Your Inspiration; Dragon Images; All About Space; FashionStock.com*
p. 256 Annette & Christian, Living4media.co.uk; *traumschoen*
p. 257 *Pavel Sytsko; Iriana Shiyan; Alexandre Zveiger; Ovidiu Hrubaru; rehanq; Ozgur Coskun*
p. 260 José-Luis Hausmann, Living4media.co.uk
p. 261 *hifashion; PlusONE; Odrida; Jaros;* Idyll Home, idyllhome.co.uk
p. 262 *gifted*
p. 263 Boca do Lobo, Bocadolobo.com; *Algirdas Gelazius; Alexandre Zveiger; pbombaert; LIU ANLIN;* Henri Del Olmo, Living4media.co.uk
p. 264 Annette & Christian, Living4media.co.uk
p. 265 *GoodMood Photo; Sam Aronov; 2M media; Africa Studio; jan1982*
p. 266 *Marko Poplasen*
p. 267 Tulikivi Kide 2 Fireplace White by Tulikivi2012 - Own work. Licensed under CC BY-SA 3.0 via Wikimedia Commons, Commons.wikimedia.org/wiki/File:Tulikivi_Kide_2_Fireplace_White.jpg#/media/File:Tulikivi_Kide_2_Fireplace_White.jpg; *paultarasenko; saschanti17; Jodie Johnson; WorldWide; Vladzimirska Svyatoslava*
p. 268 *stockernumber2,*
p. 269 *lev radin;* Peter Kooijman, Living4media.co.uk; *Anna Hoychuk; melis; T30 Gallery; pics721; ladie_c*
p. 270 *Alexandre Zveiger*
p. 271 *chrishumphreys; Ben Bryant; Tinxi; Oleg Malyshev; FreeBirdPhotos; Chris15232; Lorna Roberts; NinaMalyna*
p. 272 View Pictures, Living4media.co.uk; *Tinxi*
p. 273 *happydancing; Yvonne von Oswald, Living4media.co. uk; Antonius Egurnov; WorldWide; BRABBU, brabbu.com; TaraPatta; hifashion*
p. 274 Peter Kooijman, Living4media.co.uk
p. 275 *Andrey Bayda; Maria Sbytova; FashionStock.com; All About Space; iOso; IVASHstudio*
p. 276 *Great Stock!, Living4media.co.uk*
p. 277 Annette & Christian, Living4media.co.uk; *FashionStock.com; Maria Sbytova; SvetlanaSF; All About Space; indira's work; PlusONE*
p. 278 Radoslaw Wojnar, Living4media.co.uk; *Neangell*
p. 279 *FashionStock.com;* Radoslaw Wojnar, Living4media. co.uk; *Simone Becchetti, Stocksy.com; fiphoto;* Interior Design: Builders Design, Builder: KB Home, Buildersdesign.com; *Andrei Zveaghintev*
p. 280 Tom Meadow, Living4media.co.uk
p. 281 *Mikhail_Kayl; karamysh; WorldWide; Elena Schweitzer; Yulia Grigoryeva; FashionStock.com; David Papazian*
p. 282 *Great Stock!, Living4media.co.uk*
p. 283 *PlusONE; Chris15232; Andreja Donko; Agnes Kantaruk; mythja; Nata Sha*
p. 284 Emily May, Gohausgo.com
p. 285 *Photographee.eu;* Emily May, Gohausgo.com; *SARYMSAKOV ANDREY; patsy&ulla,* Living4media.co.uk; *Photographee.eu; Nattle; AC Manley*